W9-DAW-589

FRENCH PHILOSOPHERS IN CONVERSATION

This collection of conversations eavesdrops on contemporary themes in French intellectual life. The short question-and-answer format of the dialogue provides an ideal introduction to the often daunting work of modern French philosophers. Such well-known figures as Jacques Derrida, Luce Irigaray, Emmanuel Levinas and Michel Serres are joined in this book by thinkers whose writings are only now begining to make an impact on the English-speaking world: Michèle Le Doeuff and Monique Schneider.

In a readable and accessible way Raoul Mortley has drawn out the ideas, personalities and society of these interesting and important thinkers. Each thinker represents one or more strand of the Parisian philosophical scene, and feminism, phenomenology, literature, semiotics, psychoanalysis and communication are just some of the many subjects covered in this book.

French Philosophers in Conversation will appeal to everyone interested in modern thought and the major impact thinkers from France continue to have. This is a genuinely 'friendly' book which introduces an interesting and potentially difficult area to the widest possible audience.

Raoul Mortley is Dean and Professor of Philosophy at the School of Humanities, Bond University, Australia. He spent nearly a decade in France studying the history of philosophy and was at one time the Director of Research in Philosophy at the Centre National de la Recherche Scientifique in Paris. During this period he researched and conducted the interviews which constitute this book.

FRENCH PHILOSOPHERS IN CONVERSATION

Levinas, Schneider, Serres, Irigaray, Le Doeuff, Derrida

Raoul Mortley

London and New York

First published 1991
by Routledge
11 New Fetter Lane, London EC4P 4EE

Simultaneously published in the USA and Canada
by Routledge
a division of Routledge, Chapman and Hall, Inc.
29 West 35th Street, New York, NY 10001

© 1991 Raoul Mortley; chapter 4 © 1991 Luce Irigaray
Typeset in 10/12pt Palatino by
Selectmove
Printed and bound in Great Britain by
T.J. Press (Padstow) Ltd, Padstow, Cornwall

British Library Cataloguing in Publication Data
Mortley, Raoul
French philosophers in conversation: Levinas, Schneider, Serres,
Irigaray, Le Doeuff, Derrida
1. French philosophy
I. Title
194

Library of Congress Cataloging in Publication Data
French philosophers in conversation: Levinas, Schneider, Serres,
Irigaray, Le Doeuff, Derrida, Raoul Mortley
p. cm.
Contents: Emmanuel Levinas – Monique Schneider – Michel Serres –
Luce Irigaray – Michèle Le Doeuff – Jacques Derrida.
Includes bibliographical references.
1. Philosophy, French – 20th century.
2. Philosophers – France-Interviews. I. Mortley, Raoul.
B2421.F73 1991
194--dc20 90–34899

ISBN 0 415 05254 8
0 415 05255 6 (pbk.)

CONTENTS

INTRODUCTION

The French have had a long and proud tradition of philosophy, from the medieval Sorbonne onwards. The best-known French thinker for the Anglo-Saxon world is probably Descartes, and this reflects the specific conditions of Anglo-Saxon philosophy: but seeing things through the French education system one would gain a different impression.

Philosophy is part of the literary culture of this most literate of peoples: it reaches the general reading public and penetrates the educational scene more deeply than in other countries. Philosophy is taught in senior secondary schools, and the names of the well-known philosophers are known by people quite removed from the world of institutional education.

It is virtually impossible to capture the tenor of six figures as diverse as those represented in this book. But it is clear that contemporary French philosophy in general has a reputation for radicalism. It is true that many continue to work in a Cartesian way, that is in the rigorously logical and analytic way characteristic of Descartes, but these are not the names that have become well-known abroad. It is in the issues addressed, and the manner in which they are treated, that contemporary French philosophy seems to whet the appetite. The critics are many: 'facile and superficial' is the description of contemporary French philosophy by a contemporary French philosopher. 'Theatrical' is the term chosen by an eminent German philosopher. And it is true that the outsider can be struck by the attention to style, to demeanour, and to public persona, which characterizes (and characterized) some contemporary practitioners. There is also the arcanum style, by which obscurity and mysteriousness serve to bolster the sense of an organized sub-group to which only the initiates belong. It is easy to be disgraced.

Thus the social face of contemporary French philosophy is worthy of a study in itself. But there is real substance to be found, despite the flair, and one point that must be made is that French philosophy has always been closer to literature than it has been in English-speaking countries. The *salon* is different from the common room as a place for interaction, and different in respect of those whom it brings together. Sartre wrote both works of philosophy and novels, as well as works which are both literary and philosophical at once: *Words*, his autobiographical work, is an example of the latter. Michel Serres, who is interviewed in this book, combines perfectly the philosophical and the literary in *Les Cinq Sens*, which was awarded a literary prize in Paris in 1986 (see Chapter 3). The literary conscience weighs heavily in French philosophy: the link between the two disciplines is thought to be natural and important. Some remarks made by Monique Schneider (see Chapter 2) seem to count against this, but this is about a specific context, and it is generally true that the philosopher in contemporary France pays more attention to the art of seduction and attraction than does his/her equivalent in Britain or America. It is this very aspect of French philosophy which appeals to students, and to a broader social group than is normally the case.

The relationship between philosophy and literature in the mainstream Anglo-American tradition could be described as one of mutual suspicion: philosophers see their discipline as being about knowledge and truth, and that of the *littérateurs* as being about feelings. Literary people see philosophy as diverting into analytic byways, failing to deal with the existential and the subjective. This is the subject of a whole debate in philosophy, but it should be noted that, as Michel Serres points out, from the outset Plato has the two sides in one person: the logician of Parmenides co-existing with the winged charioteer of the *Phaedrus*, which is a dialogue about inspiration, of both a literary and philosophical kind. It is no accident that this dialogue is more or less omitted from discussion in English-speaking philosophy departments, or from the study of Plato, whereas it is well established in French scholarship. The role of the imagination in philosophy is addressed much more in France than it is in Britain. Gaps in the philosophy curriculum point to a state of affairs in philosophy itself: the absence of Neoplatonist studies in both Britain and America is matched by its presence in France and, to a lesser extent, Germany and Italy. The names of certain Platonist philosophers, such as Damascius, do not even appear in standard reference works in Britain, whereas they are given many pages in equivalent French works. And these Neoplatonists, such as Plotinus and Damascius, deploy a kind a speculative intuitive method in metaphysics, which we see at work in the continental tradition. A study of the institution of philosophy and in particular the curriculum in the various countries will reveal many implicit philosophical statements being made, and often these are statements of the most important and fundamental kind. As is often the case in philosophy, the fundamental principle remains hidden; what underlies these curriculum choices is a set of claims about priorities and method in philosophy.

It is clear that English-speaking philosophy is closer to science than is French philosophy. The exception here is Michel Serres, who is consciously involved with scientific method and progress: interestingly, he is also one of the most literary of the group selected for this book. (This would be no surprise to Lucretius.) There are others actively involved with both philosophy and science: Michel Paty, both physicist and philosopher, is one who works in the philosophy of science in the Anglo-American sense. But he and others like him constitute a minority and do not get the fanfare and attention of those represented in the present book. By and large, French philosophy does not link itself with science in the areas of physics, artificial intelligence, or in methodological questions; in the matter of biology, however, the position is somewhat different. Nor is the kind of regular conjunction of physics and philosophy or mathematics and philosophy which is found in Anglo-Saxon philosophy found so much in France.

The most important influences on French philosophy at the present time are German. The three 'Hs' are well-known as the preparatory diet: Hegel, Husserl and Heidegger. Most of the group interviewed in this book read German more than they do English: to the names above, we should of course add those of Nietzsche and Freud, and these five provide a genuine context for the development of French philosophy. The entry of Heidegger into the French world is discussed by Levinas, who himself played an important role in this process. Heidegger is identified with both left and right in France, through different extensions of his work. His apparently pro-Nazi sympathies placed him in the dubious category for many years after the war, although in present-day Paris he is very widely read. Levinas, and also Beaufret, are the two names most associated with the importation of Heidegger into France from Freiburg. Hegel's route was partly through forms of Marxism, and partly through an influential teacher in Paris, Koyré. Husserl and phenomenology came with the influence of Heidegger.

One of Derrida's seminal works, *Differance* (in *Margins of Philosophy*) is developed very much in response to a structure established by both Hegel and Heidegger. This is partly the French method – of beginning from a text and philosophizing from there into new areas – but it is clear that the starting-point is the German tradition. A sensationalist book appeared in 1985, by Alain Renaut and Luc Ferry, entitled *La Pensée 68*, which claimed that all that was famous in contemporary French philosophy was but German philosophy dressed up: Foucault, Althusser, Derrida, Lacan, Deleuze – all the big names are included. Foucault is categorized under 'le nietzschéisme français', and Derrida under 'l'heideggerianisme français'. A kind of reductionist exercise is carried out in the interests of a socio-political statement rather than a serious analysis, and a real point is overemphasized. There is little point in saying dramatically that Athenian philosophy was really Eleatic, or stolen from Samos, because Plato stood in the position of responding to and developing Parmenides and Pythagoras. These revelations have an obviousness about them. But there is a point to remember, and that is that most French philosophers, if they know any foreign language, probably know German before they know English.

This particular legacy means that ontology is very important in contemporary writing. There is a certain very traditional side to Heidegger which has echoes of Thomism, and which reaches right back to Parmenides: the fundamental question is perceived to be about the nature of being, in what it consists, and how it conducts its existence. The concern of Heidegger for Being, and Being-there (*Sein*, *Dasein*) is well-known: Hegel describes a saga of Being which resembles a historicizing of Parmenides' Being, which is no longer immobile and timeless, but evolves and develops in a kind of *Pilgrim's Progress*.

The spectre of a hidden world of being, obscure but full of authenticating presence, is a fundamental influence in the French philosophical world. It comes into the Hegelian reading of Freud provided by Lacan, and is the most important element in the filling out of Freud's ideas into a philosophical theory. The presence or absence of the phallus can then come to point to a presence or absence of being in the sense described above: the idea of 'lack' can receive a full development in what are virtually cosmic terms. This conflation of the different streams has given Freudian theory a great impetus in Paris, and is responsible for the specific character which it has there. It leads to a universalization of Freud into all the areas of existential concern, and a reading of him in terms provided by the existentialist writers.

The psychoanalytic philosophy of Monique Schneider has its affinities with the Lacan school, but she pays attention to matters which are not the habitual fare of the French. Her analysis of language, cast in the ontological-cum-psychoanalytic framework which we have observed, is based on a mixture of Wittgenstein, Freud and other insights. She is more *analytic*, in the British sense, within her own framework. By the same token she is very conscious of the symbol and of meaning: there is a strong semiotic strand in the ontological substrate of her work. The images of Freud are used to explain him: what is inexplicit in his text is highlighted in the quest for explanation.

The phenomenological method, of describing being as it really is and as it really appears, is most clearly present in Levinas. But it must be said that this kind of approach is everywhere in the type of contemporary French philosophy to which we refer. A kind of step-back, look, and an attempt at redescribing what is and what emerges, is a common manoeuvre: this clearly has its links to the phenomenological tradition. And equally close to that tradition is the sense that the essence of being may be hidden, subject to some arcanum principle, and that our ordinary construction of reality will have to be reconstructed on the basis of a speculative act of the imagination. This last point should be emphasized, since the reconstruction of the ordinary perception of reality is what the scientist does in day-to-day investigation and theorizing. But here, the kind of new look at reality which takes place is a product of the metaphysical imagination, and this brings us back to the proximity of the literary in French philosophy. The creative act of the philosophical imagination is not so different from that of the literary or poetic imagination.

The focus on the imagination is itself an important theme. Thus Michèle Le Doeuff (see below), who has many strings to her bow, pursues the enquiry into the philosophical imagination in all aspects of her work. Her view is that metaphors and images, and their absence, tell much about the real basis of the philosophical writing in question. This is not unlike the theory that attaches to the role of paradigms or models in the thinking process, which forms part of the Anglo-Saxon philosophy curriculum. But there are important differences: first, the *imaginaire* is not merely indicative of driving modes of thought, but is often a sign of unconfessed and dissimulated ideas. Second – and Le Doeuff focuses on these – it is the gaps in the philosophical discourse which may be more revealing than the continuous text. Thus if an author interrupts his narrative to recount a dream (the *somnium doctrinae* of one of her articles), then the interruption may be more telling than the main text itself. And it is telling not just about the author's specific frame of mind but about knots which remain to be untied in the systematic form of what is being expounded. Again there is the sense of something hidden: that the ostensible agenda is not the real agenda.

This arcanum principle then, that the hidden is the essence, is one of the chief distinguishing features of such philosophy. It is in stark contrast to the respect for the formal and the explicit which characterizes the analytic tradition, whereby the real game is said to be the overt game, the one which all parties ostensibly agree to be the real game. It is rather like a court-case in which the lawyers and all orthodox observers agree that the legal contest is what is at stake, whilst the parties involved see themselves in an entirely different struggle. Some kind of 'real' issue may be involved, such as the settling of old scores, and the law may be the mere instrument of this concealed issue. A kind of charade is carried out, in which from time to time there emerge hints of what is really at stake. (And of course the charade and the real are not on entirely separate tracks, since they tend to have an involving effect on each other.)

Luce Irigaray represents an increasingly strong voice in the philosophy of human relations: her particular feminism turns on what may be said to be the legitimate difference between men and women. Opposing the homogenizing tendency which characterizes some feminism, Irigaray looks both for fraudulent attempts to characterize difference, and for sound qualitative descriptors. The discourse provided below in response to certain written questions illustrates both the conspiracy to agree on certain false characterizations of femininity, and the way in which women may accept and internalize such judgements: the flight of women from taking the subject's position in the sentence is an example of this.

The themes of difference, identity and opposition are often linked in some way. Feminism raises the issue of the tendency to polarize, to conduct thought by setting up oppositions, rather than identities or relations. The question of difference, which Irigaray teases out over and over again in different ways, is a very traditional one. For Aquinas, difference is the ground of relations, and does not stand in opposition to identity. This goes back to *alteritas* and *heterotes* in Roman and Greek philosophy, and eventually back to Parmenides and the Pre-Socratics: how can difference coexist with being? How can an entity be, if it harbours difference with itself? What is the relation of the unity in a thing, to the difference which is also present. These are urgent issues in French philosophical writing, and they find expression in social philosophy and metaphysics alike.

The issue re-emerges with Derrida's idea of 'differance', which substitues an 'a' for the usual 'e'. This is Derrida's way of signalling an enquiry into the real process of differing. Starting from an active sense of the adjective 'different', and basing his enquiry in the traditional French manner on a text to be clarified (in this case Koyré on Hegel), Derrida looks for a sense of 'differing' which lies between the active and the passive. A temporal meaning is discovered: in French 'différer' means both to delay and to refer. The process 'differance' is that by which a delaying/referring action takes place, such that 'differance' becomes the axis of language, the way it works. Language works not by a series of rigid edicts handed down by its authors, who move it about at will and with total control over it. It works rather by itself, in being in this differing process. Quite simply, 'differance' refers to the generation of a series of relations, which is in fact the consequence of common-or-garden difference. This discussion develops in the context of the ontology of Hegel, Nietzsche, Heidegger, Saussure and the ancient Greeks ('Differance', in *Margins of Philosophy*): its effect on literary theory is well-known, because it ascribes a kind of self-sufficiency to text. Text 'differs': the difference among words gives birth to that process which relates them, and weaves them into patterns. And this process is in language itself, which thereby creates its own meaning. The subject is not the prime mover as author, or reader if it comes to that. And this leads to another common theme: the disestablishment of the subject. The score is still being settled with Descartes in the French tradition.

RAOUL MORTLEY
Bond University
January 1990

Emmanuel Levinas was born in Lithuania in 1905, though he received a French university education, at Strasbourg. From here, as a student, he travelled to Freiburg where he heard both Husserl and Heidegger lecture. Through his Jewish background he knew Yiddish, and therefore enough German to comprehend the lectures of the two Freiburg philosophers: it was through this social coincidence that a conduit was created from Germany to Paris. As a philosopher in Paris, Levinas introduced and developed phenomenological themes, and became an immensely important influence, widely respected amongst younger philosophers. His institutional career was based on his position as Professor of Philosophy at the Sorbonne (Paris IV); now in his eighties, he has exercised a growing influence in his retirement. His work has evolved considerably in recent years. He suffered under the Nazis, and his work has always had a strong Jewish aspect: especially lately he has become a conscious philosopher of Judaism.

1

EMMANUEL LEVINAS

RM: You're known as a philosopher working within the pheno-
    menological tradition, but I'd like to ask about your training
    from the very beginning. You were born in Lithuania.

EL: I was born in Lithuania, where I had an education based
    on the Russian culture; even after the 1914–18 war there were
    secondary schools where teaching was in Russian. I was
    greatly influenced by Russian literature, which has been
    very important to me, and I don't forget it today in spite
    of all my western wonderments. Then I came to Strasbourg,
    where I did a year of Latin, and I took philosophy as part of
    my work towards the *Licence* degree in the French system.
    I did psychology, sociology, ethics – general philosophy and
    the history of philosophy. I then wanted to move quickly into
    personal research, and I became interested in Husserl: I got
    interested in Husserl by chance. Someone was reading a book
    of his next to me.

RM: So it didn't come from your formal French training?

EL: Not at all: there I did modern philosophy, contemporary
    philosophy, and there it was Bergson. And so a love of Bergson
    has remained with me all my life, though now of course he has
    been somewhat forgotten. And I would never have been able
    to bring together my interest in Heidegger if I hadn't had the
    prior training in Bergson. Of course, at that time Heidegger's
    name was completely unknown: it was 1928. So I read Husserl,
    I was very taken by his logic, I read his *Ideas* and I wanted to go
    and hear him in Freiburg. So I went there to attend his lectures:
    he had just retired but he was still teaching, and during this
    summer semester of 1928 we heard the name of his successor
    – it was to be Heidegger. So, as you can imagine, Heidegger

11

came with many of his students from Marburg, and, with him alongside Husserl, it was the place where one felt one was getting the last word in philosophy.

RM: So Freiburg was an important philosophical centre: but of course it's even now a very small town.

EL: But in Germany small towns are very important; great philosophical movements carry the names of small towns. There's no Berlin school: but there's Heidelberg, Marburg, Freiburg.

RM: And you learnt German?

EL: Well of course I had learnt German since childhood . . .

RM: At high school?

EL: Yes at high school, but being Jewish we spoke Yiddish, so I had a good grounding in German. I read a great deal in German and so there was no language problem then. I became enchanted with Heidegger and his *Being and Time*, and I still think very highly of it: there are only five or six books like this in the history of philosophy. I am much less attracted by the late Heidegger, everything that's coming out now in the *Ausgabe*, which I know less well in fact, but Husserl's phenomenology as it emerges in Heidegger is still very illuminating to me.

RM: So it was virtually chance which led you to Husserl?

EL: Yes it was, and I felt immediately that there was here a generally new look at philosophy. I thought of it as the last statement on philosophy, and I attach great significance to that sentiment: and so I came to admire greatly the possibilities of Husserl's phenomenology, of developing it through the thought of Heidegger.

RM: The course of your career is rather different in French terms, in the sense that there couldn't have been many French students who went to Freiburg. And of course for some time Heidegger was frowned on in France because of his apparent connection with Nazism.

EL: Ah that . . .! I don't know whether it was apparent, but in any case that was afterwards. At that earlier stage nothing of the kind was weighing on him. He was relatively unknown: there was very little information on Heidegger in France. Heidegger was discovered later, during the war. Sartre and Merleau-Ponty were involved and since then, of course, a considerable Heideggerian following has established itself in France.

RM: It seems to me to be an important fact that in France it was only a part of *Being and Time* that was published.

EL: It's still the case . . .

RM: But I think that Gallimard is bringing out the rest . . . [now published]

EL: And there's a big quarrel about all that (*laughter*). You know that in France, and this is very interesting for foreigners, there are classes after the final year of high school, special classes after the *baccalauréat*, the *hypocagne*, which offers training for the Grandes Ecoles, and there was a teacher in this system called Beaufret: a whole series of former high school students learnt Heidegger from him at this level. It's unique really.

RM: It's clear also that there is a current of Jewish thought which has been influential in your own work. Did you have a formal training in this area?

EL: I learnt Hebrew and biblical texts, and studied modern Hebrew from my childhood. From the age of 6 we had a special teacher for this purpose. But that was the Bible. I didn't know anything about the background of the Talmud and the Rabbinic commentaries. I took this seriously only at a very much later stage, and it was in Paris that I undertook study in this area, privately, and I made contact with a teacher of exceptional skill, quite remarkable, and I often describe our encounter. He taught me a disciplined way of reading these texts – the way to find complex things beneath things which are apparently innocent – and even within terribly tangled things.

RM: So you already knew Hebrew well at that stage?

EL: Classical Hebrew of course, but the Talmud is partly in Aramaic. This was an important stimulus to me: I am not talking about religious enthusiasm, though I am not attacking that. The essential thing was the invitation to *think* that I found in these documents. Among my publications there is a whole series of works drawn from this, but I never run together my general philosophy with what I call the more confessional writing. I don't have the same publisher: the confessional writings are published with Minuit. But there's certainly some infiltration from one side to the other.

RM: On your method in philosophy, if I may ask you an Anglo-Saxon type of question, how would you distinguish your approach from the empirical approach? What are the essential traits of empiricism?

EL: I know empiricism in its traditional form. But I've never studied analytic philosophy with its linguistic empiricism. My method is phenomenological; it consists in restoring that which is given, which bears a name, which is objective, to its background of intention, not only that intention which is directed towards the object, but to everything which calls it to concreteness, to the horizon. I've often said that it is research into the staging [*mise en scène*] of that which is the object; the object which, left to itself, is clarified, as much as it closes off the gaze – as if the giving was like an eyelid which lowers itself as an object appears, and consequently as if the objective is always abstract. Concreteness is the ensemble of what is lived, of intentionality, which is not entirely heuristic; it includes the axiological and the affective. Consequently meaning is given in this concreteness, and there can be surprises here over the general role of thematization.

RM: And in this schema, or to take the Heideggerian term you used a moment ago, in this horizon, what is the place of the mind? Does the mind . . .

EL: I don't know what you mean by mind: is it the objective mind, objective thought?

RM: I mean the capacity of the subject, the knowing subject, within the framework of the real, and I want to refer too to the subject/object distinction.

EL: I think they are inseparable, not through intentionality, which is an essential moment of the subject. Thought is not purely intentionality; I wanted to come back to that, not purely because of Husserl's idea of the eidetic data. That is not for me the essential break with intentionality. But on intentionality I am rather inclined to think that being, what is given, what imposes itself – that the position or statement, the fact that it shows itself, is like an emphasis of its own being. And when I use the expression that it *shows* itself, of course it does so in the being of the subject, concretely. It is also presupposed that it appears in truth and that this truth is *affirmed*. So that what you call mind, on the subjective side, is for me an essential moment of the positioning itself, of being.

14

As if the fact that showing itself was the emphatic moment of the positioning of itself. It is the intentional co-relation, and the very concreteness of being. But the question is whether the positioning of being is the essential feature of thought. Insofar as being is the primary philosophical occurrence, I've no great difficulty in grasping that there is a thinking which thinks it: there is the act, and for it the fact of emerging in truth, and its affirmation in being, its positioning, is in fact the act of thought which affirms it as present, in presence. So, in this case, being itself is essentially presence. And it is very easy to show that that which is a memory is re-presentation, and that which is not yet is intentionally anticipated. In any case being is presence, and in this case the mind is that which welcomes it. The mind welcomes it because it shows itself as presence and affirms itself as presence to thought. So I hesitate over the appearing within this being which positions itself, which is the world, rest. Rest, presence, it's the same thing – it's there. There can take place here the encounter of faces, human faces, where instead of this affirmation, this rest, you are called, or you undergo two apparently contradictory things: the appearance of weakness, which does not affirm itself – a kind of mortality. Mortality is in no way *my* death, but the death of the other. But there is not only weakness; at the same time as this weakness appears in the face – this mortality – there appears also the command: do not leave me in solitude. Consequently, there is an imperative, which is in no way the imperative of the universal which arouses my will: on the contrary there is an authority in the face, which commands me not to leave this mortal to dwell alone. Taking up that: here is my responsibility for the other.

RM: The idea of the face, what is it exactly? I am thinking here of the Greek term *prosopon*, with its ambiguity, in that it means both face and mask. The face could be a veil before the person.

EL: The face is always given as countenance. We meet this countenance in the look of the other, and it doesn't declare itself: but behind it there is the weakness. If there were only the mask, if it were only the countenance which was given, there would only be a mask. I don't understand it in the Greek sense: the weakness is in fact unveiled, I would even say it's naked. There is a nudity revealed: *Enthüllung*, 'disclosure', is a state without shame; there is the moment in the human face which is the most naked and exposed state of human experience. Being is always exposed to consciousness: here it's the mortal which is shown. Inevitably, together with this, there is also the command, or the imperative: do not leave me in solitude. You can't abandon the other person. There is a Hebrew expression: 'Here am I'; it's used by Abraham. And the word which sums up this positioning is *responsibility*. The look is always 'to hand' of course, *zu Hand*; there is a dominance in the look, a technical dominance. But here I am talking about the relation of obligation, and responsibility. One can use the term 'hostage' here: I am the hostage, because I am responsible. Not because I have participated in some past or other, in which I have done something. There is the revelation of a past which has never been present, in which I am, through my responsibility, obligated to anyone who turns up.

RM: The idea of one's responsibility to the other, and to some extent the idea of the face, presuppose an otherness, an alterity, within being, and I think you have been among those who have objected to the reduction of being to sameness.

EL: Otherness is present from the consciousness onwards. Intentionality provides for something which is other and which offers itself to you, or which is given to you – which lends itself to possession and domination. Objects and things, when they are seen, are grasped. This is pursued in the *Begriff*, the taking up: but here the idea of grasping is not present. When I talk about responsibility and obligation, and consequently about the person with whom one is in a relationship through the face, this person does not appear as belonging to an order which can be 'embraced', or 'grasped'. The other, in this relationship of responsibility, is, as it were, unique: 'unique' meaning without genre. In this sense he is absolutely other, not only in relation to me; he is alone as if he were the only one of significance at that moment. The essence of responsibility lies in the uniqueness of the person for whom you are responsible. You are in love, a love without concupiscence, along the lines of Pascal's idea, and love in this sense is access to the unique. And here is the otherness involved. Furthermore, the 'I' which finds itself with this responsibility cannot be replaced. Consequently within this exceptional relationship between me and the other, he who is responsible is the chosen one. It's the uniqueness of the elect. So, apart from what we called mind at the beginning, the mind which knows and embraces, which invests, which possesses, uses, which takes, understands – all this activity of the mind is in complete contrast to the idea of the self which is passive, under obligation and unique. Consequently, there is the order of knowledge, and on the other hand the responsibility for the other, which is a strange, or foreign, thing, within being. Being is itself continuance or persistence of being within its own being: so you have here a being which is *for* the other. For the other: within the human there is the possibility of being for the other, which is the sphere of ethics, and this is the order of holiness. You can talk about holiness without being holy, of course (*laughter*): very few men are saints, but no man questions sanctity. If sanctity is questioned, it is in the name of another sanctity. Consequently, human nature is not conceived in the light of its position as subject against the world, but in the light of this appeal, this order, which is primary. The position of the thinking self, the transcendental ego which knows, synthesizes, gathers together, embraces, possesses: I wonder if its very uniqueness is not the culmination of an ethical operation, in which it establishes itself as unique. So there are not two modes of the mind, but there is a priority in itself of ethics, or of holiness in relation to the quality of *need* of the world to be possessed.

RM: Holiness is difference, in relation to the ordinary or the profane, so to speak?

EL: I am not talking about religion: it's not a religious analysis I am giving. I am not talking about the sacred: the sacred is the ambience in which holiness often dwells, but they are not the same thing. I have published a little collection of Talmudic writings which is called *From the Sacred to the Holy*: the sacred is the easy way of avoiding holiness itself.

RM: If we look at the idea of otherness for a moment: I have understood your interest in one's responsibility for the other, that one is *for* the other. But don't you run the risk of exaggerating the difference between people, between beings. Couldn't racism and also sexism find some reinforcement in the kind of view you advocate? You often talk about the feminine, or femininity . . .

EL: I haven't quite got to the bottom of this matter, but in the idea that the other is of a different genre . . . everything which is dispersed has the unity of him who grasps it. There is the unity of form . . . the first synthesis of the constituting self. But here, in relation to the other; it is *because* he is alien that he is incumbent on me. It's an entirely different way of coming to terms with the other. Sex itself is otherness of genre, but within a relation: so in a relationship with the feminine, a breaking of genre has already taken place. This is a very important moment in the accession to the total otherness of the face. But you ask me about exaggerating the difference: I would say in reply that there is a philosophy of human nature from the moment that there are two of us. And in fact there are three of us (*laughter*); and there is a sense in which my relationship with another is in conflict with my relationship with a third party. Consequently, I cannot live in society on the basis of this one-to-one responsibility alone. There is no calculation in this responsibility: there is no pre-responsible knowledge. The face carries everything, so in my view it is in the relationship to a third party that knowledge comes.

I often say, though it's a dangerous thing to say publicly, that humanity consists of the Bible and the Greeks. All the rest can be translated: all the rest – all the exotic – is dance.

So responsibility, which is not blind, asks: 'What is there between men?' And all the politics of the Greeks – I'll take this idea right through – emerges. Through this pity, there is a relationship of pity, we enter into knowledge, judgement and justice: I always say that justice is the primary violence.

RM: Speaking of knowledge, could I jump here to the myth of Adam and Eve. The Fall was also the acquisition of knowledge: in certain Jewish interpretations of the tale the Fall was seen as a rise, a gaining of stature for humanity, in that human beings acquired knowledge.

EL: Oh I think that the Jewish reading of it also treats it as a Fall, but there is another meaning to your question, which is the sense given to it by Maimonides. He asks how it is that knowledge, which is such a fine thing, has sprung from an error or imperfection. He says that it was *approximate* knowledge which came from the Fall, and that the first knowledge was ethical, and that it was also flawless (*laughter*): he literally says that. You can put it differently and say that it's a type of knowledge which leads to the atomic bomb, and that this knowledge came from the Fall.

Sometimes I wonder why I'm always going on about faces, if, in the end, instead of listening to God through the faces of people, you look into the heart, inspect the entrails so to speak . . . well, you reach a just society, and this just society has judges, and this society with judges has an army, and so on. And so we reach the liberal state, the state which always asks itself whether its own justice really *is* justice. This particular quality of the liberal state might appear to be a political contingency, nothing to do with metaphysics, but it is a metaphysical moment of the human phenomenon. That's very important.

RM: A moment in the progress of *Dasein*?

EL: Heidegger's *Dasein*? *Dasein* never wonders whether, by being *da*, 'there', it's taking somebody else's place! As we know, Germany has always had its *Dasein* (*laughter*). No, to return to the thing I was saying, the liberal state, with a free press . . . you know the prophets of the Bible, they come and say to the king that his method of dispensing justice is wrong. The prophet doesn't do this in a clandestine way: he comes before the king and he tells him. In the liberal state, it's the press, the poets, the writers who fulfil this role. And in second place, once justice has been applied, there is still some charity which remains. Let me tell you a story drawn from Jewish wisdom: one biblical text says: 'You shall not look at the face of the person on whom you are passing judgement.' In this context the face refers to the rank, the social class, or any particular distinction of the person being judged: you judge without regard to the person. But other texts say: 'The Eternal turns his face towards you.' Now if the Eternal turns his face towards you, he looks into your face. Which is right? He doesn't look into your face – that's before the judgement. He looks into your face – that's after the judgement (*laughter*). That's how it's solved.

RM: Why does he look afterwards?

EL: Because, once justice has been rendered, there is in fact a moment of personal contact which can soften the penalty, or the pain of it: it can soften the cruel, or the hard side of justice.

RM: So there's a kind of relationship established between the punisher and the punished.

I'd like to go now to the relationship between Judaism and philosophy: what relationship can there be between Judaism and philosophy? There have always been problems between religion and philosophy, and, in Christianity for example, the growth of Protestantism could in some ways be regarded as the rejection of philosophy within the Christian tradition. I've always been fascinated by the fact that in antiquity you have one Jewish philosopher – philosopher in the Greek mode – namely Philo, and, after him, nothing until the medieval period. Why this thousand-year void? Was Philo judged to be too adulterated from the intellectual point of view? Too Greek perhaps?

EL: The question is a little ambiguous, because by philosophy you mean a certain well-defined tradition, whose leaders we could name, the great men who established it, but which is wholly concerned with knowledge. The culmination of this sort of philosophy lies in contemplation, as in the tenth book of Aristotle's *Nicomachean Ethics*, in contemplation of pure essence. Transcending the otherness of the world, and its alien character, through a kind of knowledge which makes it accessible to human thought. Happiness itself, the aspiration of man, is thought to lie in understanding and the peace of truth. I don't know whether the word 'truth' has the same meaning in Judaism: it's biblical of course. It's common to Judaism and Christianity, the presence itself of God and association with him. His *proximity* is the concern. Maimonides and people like him talk about understanding God but they also mean association with him, proximity to him. So there is a problem about how to relate this proximity and the transcending of the otherness of material reality. It doesn't take place through knowledge, but through a relationship with the other, in love of the other. This irreducible love of the other cannot be contained in terms which are expressible in philosophy. The Jewish contribution in the history of philosophy always comes with the appearance of the ethical as being of prime importance. This is not really an explanation, but it is an attempt to grasp the sense, the *Sinn* of philosophy as sociality.

RM: Sociality?

EL: Yes, sociality. Being in society is often seen as being inferior to being one, alone. In western philosophy, sociality is regarded almost as a coincidence, which is a failure. A coincidence which failed to realize its potential: and there's a whole theme of western philosophy, and western literature as well, which is devoted to disappointment in love. Lovers misunderstand each other. They don't coincide, they are alien to each other. In my view sociality should be regarded as the excellence of the human species: sociality is worth more than solitude. And of course this idea is not my own, there are others in the history of the twentieth century who have dealt with the I/thou relationship.

RM: Buber?

EL: Yes, Buber: and Gabriel Marcel in France. And the thought of Merleau-Ponty, the idea of a rupture in the cognitive relationship with the object as being the essential for the subject. He looks always to the subject as incorporated, so to speak, in its entry into the flesh. So this subject is not solely accomplished within knowledge: that's how this biblical theme can become a philosophical one. But we can't always be sure of the 'happy ending' when we follow this line. After living through Auschwitz . . . but we must still take account of the other man. Even if taking account of him is not recompensed. There are many levels of religion . . . . But I want to say that this business of Auschwitz did not interrupt the history of holiness. God did not reply, but he has taught that love of the other person, without reciprocity, is a perfection in itself.

RM: The fact of Auschwitz is one of the most important facts of the twentieth century: do you think there is anything exceptional in it, over and above the ordinary context of European anti-Semitism?

EL: Yes, it was not a question of the number of people, it was the way, the way . . .

RM: But it's never only a question of numbers . . .

EL: Well, the number there were plenty of numbers as well: but the flesh . . . of the murdered people transported on the lorries . . . it was referred to in neutral terms – *die Scheiss* – they weren't human bodies. That was what was exceptional. It was murder carried out in contempt, more than in hatred . . .

RM: Returning to the question of Judaism and philosophy; sometimes the question is asked whether there was a Jewish science. There was a Greek science and a Greek philosophy, and among the Jews the Bible at the same time. Then a kind of encounter took place with Philo . . . is there something in the purely Jewish intellectual tradition which could be considered anti-scientific? The same question has been asked of Christianity of course.

EL: It's a question for the whole history of philosophy, but I would say this, that Greek science, its metaphysics, its logic, these are things which are compatible with Judaism, but you can't look for science in the Bible. Philo looked in the Bible for Greek metaphysics.

RM: What I mean is that there is an inaccessibility about the Talmud: it is complicated, it requires skill and training, and of course there are touches of humour . . .

EL: Oh yes, there's a lot of humour . . .

RM: . . . but you practically need to be within a tradition to appreciate it, whereas Greek science has something of the universal about it; it's a logos which is common to all.

EL: I should say this, that with the teacher I had, whose equal I have never met since, I only just penetrated the midrash, the haggadic part which tells symbolic tales. You need a great deal of imagination to read it; without that it would send you off to sleep. My teacher always used to say: 'You have to wait on your imagination.' Whatever I've written on the Talmud is based on the Haggadah, not on the *Halakha*, which is much more difficult . . .

RM: Aren't these traditions really a way of connecting the sacred text to the present?

EL: Yes . . . take for example the law of the eye for an eye, and a tooth for a tooth. That can be interpreted in the light of monetary compensation: the commentator says that compensation must be given for the lost eye. The eye has to be understood as an asset in the market-place: if an eye has been lost, the loss of work must be paid for, treatment must be paid for, the uglification, so to speak, has to be paid for. There is a whole series of things which can be settled with money. So I asked my teacher why it says 'an eye for an eye', a thing for a thing. Money existed after all – there could have been a monetary recompense. He said: 'If it didn't say that, Rothschild would have cornered the eye market.'

SELECT BIBLIOGRAPHY

Théories de l'intuition dans la phénoménologie de Husserl (Paris: Vrin 1930); English version: *The Theory of Intuition in Husserl's Phenomenology,* trans. André Orianne (Evanston: Northwestern University Press 1985).

De l'existence à l'existant (Paris: Vrin 1947); English version: *Existence and Existents,* trans. Alphonso Lingis (The Hague: Nijhoff 1978).

En découvrant l'existence avec Husserl et Heidegger (Paris: Vrin 1949).

Totalité et Infini. Essai sur l'extériorité (The Hague: Nijhoff 1969); English version: *Totality and Infinity,* trans. Alphonso Lingis (The Hague: Nijhoff 1980).

Difficile Liberté (Paris: Albin-Michel 1963).

Quatre lectures talmudiques (Paris: Minuit 1968).

Autrement qu'être, ou au-delà de l'essence (The Hague: Nijhoff 1974); English version: *Otherwise Than Being or Beyond Essence,* trans. Alphonso Lingis (The Hague: Nijhoff 1981).

Du sacré au saint. Cinq nouvelles lectures talmudiques (Paris: Minuit 1977).

De Dieu qui vient à l'idée (Paris: Vrin 1982).

Monique Schneider was born in France in 1935, and works partly in philosophy and partly in psychoanalysis. Her work is beginning to be better known, though it is still not widely read in English-speaking countries. Her major works are not translated into English. What distinguishes her writing is a rigorous analytic method, juxtaposed with an interest in psychoanalysis in the Lacan mode. Her interest in Freud goes far beyond Freud to a general philosophy of psychological states, and to an ontology of personality. Her analytic method brings her to an examination of metaphor and image which is at once carefully reasoned and imaginative. Her professional career is divided between psychoanalysis and philosophy.

2

MONIQUE SCHNEIDER

MS: Philosophy for me is an intermediate type of discipline: it is part conceptual and part literary. I like Plato a great deal: so I like to place myself at the crossroads between philosophy and a certain rhetorical style, which is quite natural – I don't recognize the separation of the two.

RM: That's interesting to Anglo-Saxons, because we don't have that literary side – at least I don't – in our philosophical training. One could almost say that our tradition of philosophy is anti-literary. English philosophical language is ugly. I've noticed that you're very attentive to your own style of writing: there is a literary tradition in French philosophy, isn't there?

MS: Perhaps not in the whole French tradition, because having a slightly literary style can be the subject of reproach both in philosophy and in psychoanalysis. Merleau-Ponty is not acceptable in some quarters because he's considered too literary, and there is something of a tradition of the severe style, as if there's some sort of obligation *not* to seduce by your writing, when you're dealing with important issues. It's true of philosophy to some extent, though it's less strong here than in Germany . . . but in psychoanalysis the obligation not to seduce by one's writing is extremely strong, which means that very often one has to be hermetic, to create in others the feeling that they understand nothing, that some initiation ceremony is required. This hermetic environment, this severity, and the image of the psychoanalyst as grand inquisitor – these are things which I find revolting. I think it's dishonest, in that there is a process of obfuscation going on. I mean that French psychoanalysis, particularly that emanating from Lacan, is extremely inaccessible: I hear students say, as they come out of seminars, 'I didn't understand a word'. They're pleased not to have understood, because, if they haven't understood, it's because what has been said to them is very good stuff.

RM: To be obscure is a proof of quality.

MS: That's right.

RM: And a kind of guru figure is created. If you're not understood, you can become a guru.

MS: Exactly.

RM: I've formed the impression also that in Paris it is not entirely the fault of the gurus that they are gurus, but it is also the public which . . .

MS: Which requires it, yes.

RM: In respect of yourself, I wonder whether you define yourself as a philosopher or a psychoanalyst.

MS: To reply I could well refer to my own development: initially I intended to abandon philosophy in favour of psychoanalysis. Historically speaking, the relationship between philosophy and psychoanalysis in France has been quite specific. It used to be customary to insist that it was necessary to renounce philosophy or any philosophical stance in order to enter the field of psychoanalysis, like going into a convent if you like. Psychoanalysis was supposed to be totally rigorous, with a radically different language, and it was supposed to be based on an experience, an experience of an initiatory character.

RM: An arcanum.

MS: Yes, exactly. And you were supposed to speak a radically different language. So at the outset there was an element of intimidation. I had the feeling that if I wanted to talk about Freud, I had to restrict myself solely to the confines of Freud. And within the study of Freud I was surprised to see that certain problems of Freudian theory itself, the problem of pleasure, or of what knowing is, these issues which are entirely mortgaged to philosophical problems, were taken up just as they were, without being enquired into. I think that there are a great number of philosophical postulates in Freudian psychoanalysis, and that psychoanalysis is frozen rigid if one doesn't see the extent of its involvement with a philosophical background. I can give a recent example: I'm working at the moment on a course on the imaginary. I was struck by the coincidence between the position of the dialectician in Plato's dialogue the *Gorgias* and the way in which Freud presents himself as a psychoanalyst. At the metaphorical level, there is a striking continuity. In the same way as Plato enquires into the image of the rhetorician, comparing rhetoric to cosmetics – a destructive, shameful, dissimulating practice – in order to contrast it with positive activities such as gymnastics, or medicine, you find in the *Introductory Lectures on Psychoanalysis* the habit of drawing a dichotomy between psychoanalysis and suggestion; he says that suggestion is like cosmetics, as in Plato's metaphor, but that psychoanalysis is like a surgical process. You feel that there is a problem about dissimulation here, which is linked to that of the likeness, and that, for Freud, whatever belongs to likeness or resemblance, belongs to the imaginary. One is supposed to somehow strip off the imaginary, remove it, to find what is behind it in Freud's thought – namely reality. It is as if the imaginary were a sort of painting, a disguise, a cosmetic placed over reality. Now if we rule out this notion, which seems to be a view about the imaginary itself, here I'm thinking aloud . . . and if we look for another approach in Freud which is virtually blocked . . .

RM: . . . blocked in Freud himself?

MS: . . . in Freud,

RM: . . . in spite of himself?

MS: Yes, in spite of himself, as if this long cultural tradition of suspicion of the imaginary, which is seen as a double, or as a misleading appearance, prevented him from situating it in its proper place. Freud seems to be locked into a philosophical, and almost theological, notion of the imaginary, an imaginary which provides for evil, the Fall, and error; and this locking-in may have stopped him working out his own research in the field of the imaginary. If you work through the seventh chapter of *The Interpretation of Dreams*, you could give the imaginary an entirely different status, which would take us much closer to someone like Kant. Certain schemas which are outside that which is visual are inevitably there, for example the child and its relationship with the breast, and the principle of satisfaction; and also the suggestion that a Fall has taken place. The experience of the Fall is not an experience of real life. It is a structure of the spatio-temporal which is both experienced and given form by the child. Freud talks about the *Innenverwandlung*, the internal transformation. And this transformation can be seen as purely an emotional thing, affective, but it can also be seen as the child's way of designing or constructing a spatial structure capable of providing a foundation, on the basis of which the child can encounter the objects of the external world. So I would prefer to go in the direction of what Kant would call the 'schemas' of the transcendental imagination – the hidden technique. Perception in Freud cannot be understood without the supposition that beyond perception lies a mechanism which resembles that which Freud discerns in the dream. In the fulfilment of desire, where desire is at work, desire and experience together create form, a kind of matrix which gives structure to perception.

RM: Would it be true to say, then, that you began your career as a philosopher, and that in taking up psychoanalysis you felt that you could not in fact abandon philosophy? And you found a sort of continuity between the two, which you perhaps didn't expect?

MS: Yes, exactly. Exactly. I had the feeling that there would be a sort of gap, an inevitable and systematic rupture between the two. It seemed to me then that the postulation of this rupture made it impossible to restart Freud, as it were – to see his contradictions, and through them to carry out some development of his thought. My philosophical training was much longer than my training in psychoanalysis – I went as far as the Doctorate of Letters in philosophy, and worked on the problem of the relationship between representation and affect in Freud, and certain problems of an epistemological kind. For me the problem was the function of the affect within the process of knowledge itself, and I dealt with it by exposing Freud to a philosophical critique, without myself being a psychoanalyst. My transition took place gradually: I began to think that the reading of Freud was frozen, rigid, fossilized . . . that it had been brought to a halt by the psychoanalytic readings which had been given of it.

RM: And the philosophical background which you described to me a moment ago: clearly that's not in Freud, but you mean that there is implicitly in Freud a philosophy. Or perhaps it is explicit: I recall that he quotes Plato a bit. He went and read some philosophers, that is certainly true. But here you suggest developments, through the thought of Kant and others, which seem to you to be necessary developments.

MS: And which are not catered for by Freud. His attitude towards philosophy is very reticent; there's an element of fascination, but it's tinged with suspicion. He's aware of the fact, for example, that he comes close to Nietzsche in certain areas, but he says that he prefers not to read Nietzsche. With regard to Plato, and it is true that Freud quotes Plato often, he tends to quote Plato through the interpretation of somebody else. And Plato's contribution, the philosophy of love, constitutes another area in which psychoanalysis has its limits. Love is understood in psychoanalysis, and in the Freudian tradition, through a Judaeo–Christian perspective, in which love and hate are opposed; love is seen as a good thing, hate as a bad thing, and we're all unfortunately sinners, so to speak. In this way love is an ambivalent thing, tinged with hate, and it's supposed to get purified through the genital phase, in order to be rid of this element of hatred. I think that this way of looking at the problem is very unfortunate for psychoanalysis, and that it does cloud the understanding of what Freud calls *Verliebtheit*, which we could translate as 'amorous experience'. The German prefix 'ver' is of great interest because it points both to a deviation and to an experience which does actually culminate in its end. And I think that what Freud says of *Verliebtheit*, of amorous experience, doesn't sit at all well with what he says in general about love and hate: to understand *Verliebtheit* you have to go back to Plato, but not to what Freud has heard about Plato second-hand – he uses Aristophanes' speech only . . .

RM: The separation into pieces . . . he wonders if there's some primordial truth in this myth of Aristophanes, about the original humans being whole, then subsequently cut in half, with the result that love is defined as the pursuit of the lost half of oneself.

MS: Yes. I think that the blind alleys that Freud encounters in his thinking about love, which are also a problem in contemporary psychoanalysis, both being stuck in this Judaeo–Christian perspective, and which become clear in the expression 'love–hate relationship', which always involves a dichotomy – these blind alleys can be negotiated by paying a little more attention to Diotima's speech, and to the somewhat chancy birth of *eros*. Clearly *eros* is not the child of love, but the child of sleep, and if one examines the position of love in relation to its psychoanalytic duality – and we do have to say that *eros* is ambivalent in some sense – it would be quite stupid to fail to understand that the avid side of love, its hunting aspect, its active aspect, is part of its positive quality. So that if we try to purify *eros* of its ambivalent dimension, its dynamism will be destroyed. I think that it could be very useful if psychoanalysts went further into the text of Plato, and specifically into Diotima's speech, not only that of Aristophanes.

RM: You're talking about the love–hate ambivalence here: it could be said that in the Christian tradition there is no *eros*, but instead *agape*, which is completely different from *eros* – the erotic *eros*. This has been argued, and in certain Christian texts one could indeed demonstrate a clear distinction between Christian love and Platonic *eros*, and the Freudian libido as well. Perhaps in Christian mystical texts this distinction no longer holds: in Origen, for example, there is no real distinction between *eros* and *agape*. What do you think?

MS: This is an important problem, and I think it weighs very heavily on a great deal of French thought on the subject. Nygren's book, *Eros and Agape*, taken up again in *Love in the Western World* by Denis de Rougemont: these are important influences. We remain caught in an absolute dichotomy, a dualism between the true love, thought to be *agape* (even by certain psychoanalysts, especially those of thirty years ago), and *eros*, which continues to be vilified. And when Freud says 'true love', *die echte Liebe*, contrasting it with the love involved in transference, in which the patient believes that she loves the psychoanalyst, but does not 'truly' love the psychoanalyst, he has to make use of a distinction and which is in fact the Judaeo–Christian distinction and which doesn't cater for the ambiguity of *eros*, its connection with lack.

RM: May I ask you a question about the importance of psycho-analysis in the intellectual life of Paris, a thing which often appears striking to foreigners; or more exactly about the relationship which exists between philosophy and psycho-analysis in Paris. In the Anglo-Saxon tradition of philosophy Freud is dealt with from time to time – not often – but usually from the side of the philosophy of science; the question of whether his hypotheses can be called scientific in the ordinary sense might be raised, for example. There's a concern for science in this sort of approach, but in Paris the encounter between the two, between philosophy and psychoanalysis, is of a completely different character, I think.

MS: Yes, I think that there was a turning-point in the history of the thing; there is one school of French psychoanalysis, which is less well-known now but which was very dominant thirty years ago, namely that of the Institute of Psychoanalysis, which did in fact work along essentially scientific lines. But the encounter which took place in France between psychoanalysis and philosophy occurred basically because of Lacan. Whether or not one is in the Lacan camp (and I'm not entirely, though I do make use of the path that Lacan opened up), he reintroduced Heidegger but especially Hegel to the conceptual world of psychoanalysis and specifically to the problem of desire, desire for recognition by the other. So Lacan, thanks to Hegel, dragged psychoanalysis out of a positivist framework by attributing a great deal of importance, not in fact to culture itself, but to the universal: this actually bothers me. The variety of culture doesn't interest Lacan at all. It's the universal which interests him. Lacan has a vision of a symbolic order, like that to which one accedes through the Oedipus figure, but which is in fact an extension of Hegel's thought. This means an abrupt transition: you get the impression that the symbolic order is rather like the intuitions in Kant, which is a completely transcendent order, cut off from the order of the imagination and which is impure, as part of culture. There's too much of the cult of the universal in French psychoanalytic thought: salvation no longer comes from libidinal self-expression, but is rather a question of discovering the signifier, the key words which bring the individual into harmony with the universal. The universal alarms me personally.

RM: This is an important reversal in relation to Freud himself isn't it? In Paris there's a kind of filter between Freud and the reader, and the filter is Lacan. It's impossible to read Freud outside this set of influences brought about by Lacan, who in fact transformed Freud in various important ways.

MS: Yes, that's right. But there again, things move extremely quickly. Lacan has made reading Freud virtually impossible, while representing himself as the person who brought about the return to Freud. But he put himself forward as the only authentic interpreter of the writings of Freud, as if Freud spoke through him alone. But Lacan did have an indirect influence; in his many references to Freud he indirectly, sometimes involuntarily, invited his followers to reread Freud. And now you find with the fringe of the Lacan school – and these are the psychoanalysts who are of most interest to me – a tendency to rediscover psychoanalytic enquiry. They see that Lacan's reading isn't the last word, and that Freudian thought is full of questions and full of dilemmas, and that we should in some way undertake a rediscovery of it. It is true that Lacan did create the possibility of this rereading of Freud, but for the second generation, not for the first generation of the Lacan school.

RM: May I ask you a question now about the myth of Oedipus? We were talking about it a moment ago: it seems to me important that Oedipus does not know that he's marrying his mother. This is true of the real Greek myth, at any rate, and he does it almost accidentally. Not completely, but you see what I mean. And he doesn't know either that it's his father he kills; it is perhaps indeed his fault that he does these things – a kind of *hubris* in Sophocles' play – but he is ignorant of the real situation. Finding out the *truth* is the tragedy of the play. Freud seems to overturn the myth when he supposes that in the Oedipus complex one actively *seeks* union with one's mother, and that, whether consciously or not, one actually *desires* the death of one's father. In the case of the real Oedipus the situation was practically the opposite. He didn't want to do it: if he had known, he wouldn't have done it. I find it striking that Freud felt he had to use a myth which he turned upside down. Why use the myth at all? Perhaps there's a more fundamental question here about myth in Freud. What do you think about this desire to establish a mythical setting for his psychoanalytic views?

MS: I think that the function of myth in Freud is extremely ambiguous: I refer here to Freud's self-analysis because it's important to note the moment at which Freud has Oedipus speak, and encounters Oedipus and the myth itself. Freud's relationship to the myth is one of ignorance: he does not wish to see that Oedipus did not know what he was doing when

32

he killed his father and married his mother, and the failure to acknowledge that fact is fundamental in his own self-analysis. There is a whole series of images: darkness, chest, enclosure, burial, not-seeing. It seems to me that Freud in some way identified himself with Oedipus on the basis of the end of the play, of Sophocles' play. I think that the encounter of Freud and the myth of Oedipus took place on the theatrical level, and in the context of the distancing implied by theatre, and not through the reading of the myth itself. Freud saw a re-presentation of the theme, and *this* had a catalysing effect on him: one might refer here to Rousseau's critique of the theatre – there is a distancing effect. It would seem that Freud identified in the first place with the blinded Oedipus. I'm thinking here of the theme in his work which touches on the one-eyed, the empty eye, the absent eye, the blind eye, and so on. So in a sense it's not surprising that he wasn't able to read the Oedipus myth in its real terms; what he took from Oedipus was the idea of not knowing. What strikes me also in the Oedipus play is that it's not just any old myth involved, but one which is entirely based on the search for truth, through the search for love – and in fact now I'm wondering about the reason for this link between the myth and tragedy of truth and the whole myth of love, or tragedy of love. Myths of love, and the tragedy of love, don't interest Freud: he confesses this indirectly in the *Observation on Transference Love*, where he tells us that the love of the patient is like a theatrical performance which is suddenly interrupted by a fire. So love comes on the scene like the fire which breaks out on the stage of the theatre: it's an interruption. While Freud is interested in the character of Oedipus, he's also fascinated by Hamlet, both characters of the most tragic kind, who belong to tragedy rather than myth, and the tragedy involved is about the search for something. Both characters will undertake a search for an objective truth, which is in some way obscured; the heroes ask themselves very few questions about what they are experiencing. And on the fascination with myth, in my view Freud has given expression to the myth in a way which is virtually the negation of myth; Oedipus is of course condemned to exile. This is not mentioned, nor the question of Oedipus' childhood, in which he is practically condemned to death. Oedipus the child fails to interest Freud. Freud hears

Oedipus only when he appears to be master of his destiny, the subject of certain acts. He misses out on the infanticide at the outset, and the element of matricide, that of bringing about the fall of the sphinx – it's of course *'die' Sphinx* in German, as in Greek, a feminine word, whereas in French it's *'le' Sphinx* – and there's Jocasta hanging herself, so there is an element of matricide. In the end Freud only wished to recognize that in the myth of Oedipus which corresponded to the words of the oracle. The oracle says that Oedipus will kill his father and wed his mother, but the oracle is seen in some sense as the mythical prefiguring of the scientific word. It gives a sort of absolute statement, of a profoundly penetrating truth, which obscures momentarily the total extent of the myth itself, and its relationship to other myths. Marie Delcourt makes the connection between the myth of Oedipus and the myth of Orestes, for example: as soon as you deal with the mythical a whole new dimension is opened up, since the myths are interrelated. And Freud didn't want to know anything about the 'mythical' in that sense, in its obscure or hidden dimension. He identified with the presence of Oedipus in the first instance and he protected himself against the threat of this powerful presence, so to speak, by clinging to the security of the oracle's authority, the equivalent of the positivist truth of science, which is a kind of discourse we're familiar with from the Greeks onwards.

RM: Yes, I see why you say that Freud's use of the myth practically negates it. He chooses certain things which confirm his own tendencies: he doesn't at all embrace the myth in its full form. But there is in another sense a mythical element in Freud, even if he's not fully attuned to the Oedipus myth, isn't there? In a completely other sense, he does seek to create mythical structures of his own: the genital stage in the child has a kind of mythical staging about it. It's somewhat like the garden of Eden. He creates his own myths.

MS: Oh yes. You mean by that a myth of a progressing kind: a tale in which different dimensions are added from time to time in order to reach a kind of synthesis which allows an individual to find his own unity. A kind of eighteenth- or nineteenth-century style of myth, a modern myth.

RM: There's an incantatory element to it: one is supposed to return continually to a source, to review the myth in order to understand oneself and to develop.

MS: Yes. But at the same time what's interesting about Freud are his own contradictions: this is a way of reading him which he himself authorizes, and which psychoanalysts tend not to follow. In *The Interpretation of Dreams*, Freud, in the course of outlining his theory, says that it's only a hypothesis and that one has to be very careful not to confuse the scaffolding which he's putting up with the edifice itself. And I think that Freud will always be found to be placing himself on the scaffolding and on several scaffoldings at once . . . but where is the building? One doesn't know. Because on the question of his relationship to myth, I do think that Freud is in the process of creating a modern myth, but at the same time he feels the nostalgia for archaic myths, extremely archaic myths. For example in the research into female sexuality, Freud tells us that in order to understand the prehistory of the little girl, one has to go right back to the Minoan–Mycenaean period – so beyond even Oedipus. He feels that something's been lost, and he experiences an acute nostalgia, and I think that in one of the passages of *The Interpretation of Dreams*, a very brief one but one which I think is extremely important, he touches on something extremely significant: the birth, in the shadows, of the umbilical cord of the dream. Perhaps you can see there the return to the Delphic *omphalos*: I think that, underneath, Freud is fascinated by mythical allusions. He speaks also about the return of the shades of the Odyssey – this *is* his way of explaining the dream, through the return of Odysseus, the reference to the shades greedy for blood, coming to take the blood of the living – without being too positivist about it, you could explain the dream that way. I believe that Freud is fascinated by another level: so one can study Freud as much by trying to consolidate the edifice, making it consistent with itself, as by trying to understand the whole rite of initiation which is carried out in *The Interpretation of Dreams*. This is a magnificent construct: there's a myth here which is quite close to the myth of Genesis. At the outset Freud supposes that the child's dream is completely clear, in no way obscure: it has a pure truth about it, as if the child were in the garden of Eden. And then comes the mention of the uncle in Freud's tale, who (although he doesn't say it) seems to have led a counterfeit existence, and to have introduced falsehood into Eden. And the following chapter is about the corruption of the dream, which shows us that all our dreams are now corrupted. So all this can be interpreted as being about the intrusion of an evil character, and it can be read as a replica of the Genesis myth: at a certain point evil appears, and it is tied to deception, disguise and the figure of the fake. This is an attempt on the part of the psychoanalyst to rediscover desire, as if one could discover it within a garden of Eden, and discover it *through* a layer of falsehood.

RM: Leaving Freud and going to Wittgenstein: you've written on Wittgenstein, which is pretty rare in Paris, I suppose, and it is as both philosopher and psychoanalyst that you've dealt with his writings. What do you see as the importance of Wittgenstein for psychoanalysis?

MS: I think that Wittgenstein *should* be very important for psychoanalysis, but he's an obscure figure, hidden from view in a way: obscured by the French approach which is much too dominated by its Greek background, not so much by Plato as Platonism – the dualism of the later Platonist tradition. At a recent conference at which the philosophy of language was on the agenda, it was impossible to raise the subject of Wittgenstein: the discussion was dominated by the signifier/signified distinction, and in contemporary French psychoanalysis there is a kind of idolatry of the word, the word whether pronounced, or written down in textual form. You could say that it is in fact text idolatry which is the distinguishing feature of French psychoanalysis: we examine the discourse of a patient as if it were in textual form. Well . . . idolatry is not really the term; I should say . . .

RM: Fetishism?

MS: Yes, perhaps fetishism (*laughter*). This comes from the fact that many psychoanalysts are of Jewish origin, which is a very valuable thing in one way, because of the importance of the Jewish tradition and the mythical resonances of such figures as Abraham and Moses, for example. But there comes with it an emphasis on the sacred text, whereas the whole history of psychoanalysis attributes enormous importance to the living word, to anything resembling a language game. What interests me in Wittgenstein is that he makes it possible to activate the dualism inherited from philosophy on one side and French psychoanalysis on the other, by bringing back into the word

36

the dimension of life itself, the word itself, not the textual word. He talks a lot about breathing, or thought . . . thinking – it's like walking. Breathing, playing too: what's important in Wittgenstein is the sense of rhythm, of pulsation, the movement which animates the word. The fact that for him you escape the Greek fear of the Sirens' song; in the fear of the Sirens entertained by the ancient Greeks, and by contemporary French thinkers as well, there is presupposed a clear distinction between statement and intonation. I've been astounded to read in certain linguists: 'we must escape from the magic of intonation.' It's as if now, like Ulysses, we must once more tie ourselves up, or block our ears, in order not to hear the Sirens' song.

Wittgenstein is a philosopher who is not afraid to listen to the song of the Sirens: there are many passages in which he presents intonation not as a mode of seduction which has been superimposed on the word, as it were, but as that which enables the understanding of the message itself. So there's no trace of the dichotomy which usually functions in enquiries of this kind. And another thing that interests me in Wittgenstein is the use of certain typical word-forms, which are frequently considered, like the cry 'I'm in pain', 'something's hurting me': take the first major dream of Freud, the dream about Irma's injection. What is the first word of the dream that Freud hears in the mouth of the patient? 'If only you knew how much pain I'm in.' For Wittgenstein the question raised by such a statement is the one about the identity of the sufferer: what is the difference between the statement 'I'm in pain' and 'Ludwig Wittgenstein is in pain'? The problem he raises is that of whether there is a *subject* of pain, a subject speaking in pain. I think that it's essential to consider this at the psychoanalytic level because it makes it possible to link language and what's called the affect, or emotion. Even in Freudian psychoanalysis, too much of a distinction has been made between the statement and the affect. There is an implication that the affect can only be understood as quantity, quantity of emotion: it's supposed not have any message. In my opinion violence has been done here to the psychoanalytic *hearing* of the word: when somebody speaks, what he says is the focus of attention, and the suffering in what he says, the seductive quality of the language he uses, which penetrates everything that is said, is neglected. The suffering colours the whole of what is said. And I think this is the point sent back to Freud by the patient who says to him: 'If you knew how much pain I'm in.' It's for this reason I'm tempted to call my last book 'Father don't you see': I think that Freud, in his capacity as theoretician and interpreter of texts, disallows the childhood of language, if you like, everything about language which goes beyond the level of the text itself. Wittgenstein on the other hand allows you to re-hear the breathing element in language, everything which is genuinely alive in the text – its energy, the many gestures of intonation. So language is not locked into being nothing more than the statement it contains: on this view you can go much further than the traditional distinction between the subject of the stating and the subject of the statement. Wittgenstein enables us to go much further than the subject who makes the statement: making a statement is taken as a vital thing, and is not merely a matter of the subject.

RM: So the philosophy of language in general is very important in your view?

MS: I think that Wittgenstein is important. Austin is important too. There's another book which is infrequently discussed, by an Israeli woman who spent some time in France and who now teaches in the United States, Shoshana Felman [*The Literary Speech Act: Don Juan with J.L. Austin*, trans. Catherine Porter, Ithaca: Cornell University Press 1983], and she discusses Austin in order to bring out an aspect that male psychoanalysts often fail to recognize – the whole question of seduction. She compares Austin to Don Juan and uses Austin's writing in order to show to what extent the word plays an active role in the seduction process. French psychoanalysts in general are quite happy to accept the word as act, the idea that to say is to do, or that the word is an act: but it's only one face of the act which is recognized, and that is the imperative. That's to say the prescriptive element of the word, the hard side, which suggests order: but the seductive side – and here we're back to the Sirens – is kept entirely out of view. Austin opens up an avenue of enquiry with his idea of the implicit performative, which perhaps had already been raised by Wittgenstein; he opens up a way of introducing ethics into the word, and in France it's well accepted that there's an ethical dimension in language, together with a prescriptive or imperative element. What we do not want is the aesthetic or seductive dimension of the word. And these things can be reintroduced through the philosophy of language.

RM: Can we go to some feminist issues? There is a great deal of discussion of the role of the woman in philosophy. Progress has been made, in that many texts have been brought forward which show that there has been not only a role, or absence of one, for women in philosophy, but also an image of the feminine in philosophy, which portrays the woman as weak, lacking in rationality and so on: remarks of this kind may be found in many philosophical documents. It can be seen also that there has been a kind of difficulty on the institutional level for women: it has been practically impossible for women to become philosophers in the institutional sense, from antiquity onwards. In Plato's academy there were no women, and there were very few women philosophers in the whole history of Greek philosophy. There has been a masculine presence in philosophy, and a feminine absence, apparently. Leaving aside the social questions, about institutions, what do you think about the texture, the substance of philosophy itself? Do you think this masculinism has had an important effect on philosophy itself, on the development of philosophy?

MS: I think that is certainly true and several people have demonstrated it. At the present time there are two possible positions: defending a kind of specificity of the female word is one. A lot is said now about female discourse, as if the woman alone were able to say certain sorts of things, and as if she alone were capable of bringing forward certain new ideas. I would like to work in two different directions; to go the way of this specificity of feminine discourse, which could, I think, be linked to the connection between form and logos, and everything which is beyond form and logos. The eclipse of the woman is also the eclipse of the mother, and in the end the first step in philosophy, even if it's not expressed, is in effect the negation of one's childhood, or the sense that it must be rejected. Real philosophy is thought to be a matter of coming out of the cave, out of the state of childhood where we were before becoming men. And I think that the contribution of women is to remain sceptical about already established forms, and to place themselves in the beyond, in the very becoming

39

of forms, as they emerge from the night. I'm thinking of the text of Aeschylus, of the *Eumenides*, and the line 'O mother, my night' [l. 876]: in this transition from the nocturnal to the reign of form, to the imaginary, and to everything that's in movement – I think that here is the contribution of the feminine.

But thinking that women are the only ones who can make this contribution is to remain trapped in a masculine logic, which I would call the philosophy of the sword, the logic of the dichotomy, of difference. This is a view not shared by many feminists, of course. I think that certain male philosophers assist, perhaps, in developing a feminine theoretical perspective. I feel that Wittgenstein is close to this – obviously in certain passages more than others – because ideas are being generated with him, and are not presented in petrified form. Austin also has this side, and there is a Jewish philosopher, Emmanuel Levinas [see interview 1], whom I consider to be very important: he presents the psyche as the maternal body, and he talks about the 'elemental', where there is no object, no subject/object distinction. I think also that where there is a kind of self-scrutiny in philosophy – the possibility of discovering certain theoretical tools or certain themes which address women as well, which makes it possible to work within a *confusing* of the difference – in all these dimensions there can be a contribution which is masculine in origin.

RM: Could I ask you to define 'forms' a little more closely: the 'forms' about which you said that it might be the role of women to remain sceptical?

MS: Oh yes . . .

RM: Are they structures of thought, or dominant modes?

MS: Something instituted or established; I understand form as the procedure which permits one to establish oneself as tomb monument. In Freud, in *The Interpretation of Dreams*, scientific truth is compared in a way (it's my comparison) to a tombstone: I'm not so hostile to form, it's not a matter of being against *forms*, but of seeing from what movement, from what genesis the forms take their origin. This whole matrix, or womb, of the imagination, of the senses, of the sensitivities, enables the emergence of forms. Perhaps this is rather a personal position: I can't manage to accept psychoanalysis as it has established itself, as a monument, a tombstone; I want to get back to the originating process, to return continually to the moment of birth. So maybe I'm stuck in a birth framework, wanting to see the gestation of things, but the passion for gestation is perhaps equally as important as the passion for the institution, or the building . . . or what's circumscribed in a rigidified form.

RM: It's true that if there's too much insistence on feminine specificity, a kind of prison is created for women, and perhaps for men as well . . .

MS: I think so, yes . . .

RM: And there is another tendency, perhaps it doesn't exist in France to the same extent, towards what might be called androgynism. This is a tendency to identify the sexes, or to create a kind of mediation, a central point at which one can say that the two are the same: there are dangers in this, because difference doesn't figure.

MS: Yes, but the important thing is not to structure the problem so that it's *either* difference *or* androgynism. The androgynous idea can be of value in its critical aspect, and not only in its mythical aspect. There is a zone of confluence, and here a psychoanalytic point about male sexuality is very relevant: by seeking too much difference, Freud amputated the vision of the male sex. Perhaps it is dishonest to allude to an operation which actually took place, in which he requested that the tracts connecting the penis and the testicles be severed. For Freud the testicles have an important imaginative significance: for the man, they're the equivalent of the breasts, or of the maternal dimension of fruitfulness and creation of life. I would think it's essential, even for men, and I think that this is part of the scientific or medical imaginary at the present time, to reintroduce men into the circuit of life. To create a suture so that masculine thought is not only a matter of the phallus, or of the penis, which identifies masculinity. The idea of difference by itself mutilates both sexes. So something is at work, on the side of both men and women, and I think that if we escape the trap of dichotomous thought we can accept that there is an intermediary zone. Above all for Ferenczi who presents sexual union, or amorous behaviour, as a way of putting sexual difference at risk, in a dynamic way, for a time. So the sexes would recognize each other, each in the other, in a moment of indifferentiation, which doesn't exclude returning to a position which may be characterized by difference. I think that androgyny, and passing through androgyny, is not something to be afraid of.

RM: To conclude, could you tell us what you are working on at present?

MS: I'm taking up the trail of several things I've already touched on, but in particular I want to look at the world of tales and fables, and the question of how these are structured, by comparison with myth. There's a whole series of anonymous tales, and in the more terrifying ones everything concludes with the death of the child. These tales tend to be set aside, and I think that there is here a mode of living beyond or outside forms, being in the forest – the trip through the forest. This is a very important aspect of fables, and one doesn't see the same thing at all in myth, unless it is through the image of the labyrinth, which is, however, much more circumscribed. In this way it can be said that the hero of the fable differs from the hero of the myth, and this appears to me to be very important for the feminine imaginary, because the forest could represent the woman, if you like. It is particularly the question of time in the fable which interests me, and I want to develop this in opposition to structuralism, which tends to reject the temporal dimension. I want to explore the pulsation of the fable, its breathing, its temporality. And beyond that, I would like to investigate the origins of the feminine (*l'originaire féminin*) in relation to this separation of the maternal and the feminine, since at a certain point feminists demanded a form of emancipation which did not take account of the maternal to an adequate degree, and were even apprehensive of the notion of maternity.

I want also to look at fatherhood, and how the father can cease to be imprisoned – he's as alienated as the woman in my view – in his metaphors, rigid, vertical metaphors which cut him off from life. The 'true father' really means the one who is dead: the male is invited to see himself in terms of a model according to which he is already dead – before his birth. There's a vision of manhood, a rather final vision, which fossilizes the man. Beyond that I would like to return to the problem of the affect, or perhaps it would be better to speak of the imaginary, and the problem of what it is to become conscious *of* something, the problem of knowing. How do we gain access to knowledge? In this context Plato is very important because knowledge for him is a transformation.

RM: Yes. When you say the *'originaire'* of the woman, it's difficult to translate. I've already some difficulty with *'imaginaire'*.

MS: Oh, of course it's Athena who presides over the setting-up of things in Greece, and she had no mother. A fine passage of Nicole Loraux says 'to think that she's never known the darkness of a womb (*matrice*)'. What is it in this woman which allows her to experience herself, to recognize herself, while at the same time remaining in darkness, not knowing whether what she shelters in herself is a part of herself or a part of her mother. So the relationship to darkness, to the womb, to the belly, is very important for women, and the whole movement of the Enlightenment tended to empty out the womb. Purging the womb was necessary, if ideas were to be clarified.

RM: So the *originaire* is not the theory of origins, but the site, or the ensemble of origins . . .?

MS: The beyond the birth of form. The not-seeing woman as the equivalent of Pandora, who is in fact already a constructed form. I think that this vision of the form as it were protects against another vision of woman: when a woman is pregnant she is carrying a life, but this life she does not know. So I think it is possible to suppose that one may not know the form in itself, and this can be described as not knowing. I'm opposed to the idea of a female discourse, in which women speak about themselves as if they know who they are, as women. I think that women come to realize themselves at the moment at which they do not in fact know what they are going to bring forth. For me the relation mother–child remains captivating, and I'm greatly interested in the myth of Demeter, a myth of great power: when she loses her daughter, she does not know her form; she has simply heard a cry. Here we're back to Wittgenstein; she will travel the whole world to find her again. Where is what she's lost? What has she lost? It's something that can be reborn anywhere: every time a plant springs up from the earth, it could be her daughter. That's what I mean by the *originaire*, something beyond the established form, a kind of wandering principle, according to which one knows neither who one is, nor whom one seeks.

SELECT BIBLIOGRAPHY

Le Féminin expurgé: de l'exorcisme à la psychanalyse (Paris: Retz 1979).
Freud et le plaisir (Paris: Denoël 1980).
La Parole et l'inceste: de l'enclos linguistique à la liturgie psychanalytique (Paris: Aubier Montaigne 1980).
'Père ne vois-tu pas' (Paris: Denoël 1985).

Michel Serres was born in France in 1930, and is Professor in History of Science at the Sorbonne (Paris I). He began his adult life by training for the navy, and a love for the sea and its metaphors is always evident in his work. Originally from the south of France, Michel Serres is keenly interested in rugby. His philosophical work began with the study of Leibniz, but following this he embarked on his own self-expression, which led him to the five-volume **Hermes** *series of books. Some of Leibniz' themes persist throughout his work, particularly those concerned with combination, communication and invention. His method is based on an encyclopaedic approach, and this holism is evident in his writing: all kinds of data are held to contribute to philosophy, and the philosopher must not cut himself off from any form of investigation. His most recent work bridges the gap between philosophy and literature, and it has a wide readership.*

3

MICHEL SERRES

RM: Every year you go to Stanford to teach, in the United States; and what is it you teach there, philosophy, or the history of philosophy?

MS: I'm usually a visiting professor in the Romance Languages department, and, as you know, in America it's generally in French departments, departments of French language and literature, that it has been possible to teach philosophy of French expression. Generally what is taught under the heading of philosophy of the Anglo-Saxon countries is the philosophy of the analytic school, sometimes with a little of the history of continental philosophy, as they say. Contemporary French philosophy gets into the Anglo-Saxon countries through departments of literature.

So I was invited to the United States for this very purpose, to teach what I consider to be philosophy, within a department of literature. This doesn't bother me at all, since in a way it is a French tradition which goes right back to Montaigne, that philosophy and literature should have a productive relationship, and for this reason we don't always find it easy to classify our authors. Should Montaigne be classified as literature or philosophy? Diderot, Voltaire and so on . . . this mixture of literature and philosophy is a valuable thing.

RM: Yes: but some complain that French philosophy is too literary at the present time, that at least part of it is rather too literary in character. What do you think?

MS: Well, you can always complain about your own tongue, but your own tongue remains what it is. It is pointless to complain that Montaigne is difficult to classify, or that Diderot or Voltaire are difficult to classify, that's how it is.

It's our tradition, it's our language.

RM: It's wanting to classify at the outset . . .

MS: Exactly: that's what I mean. The difference between philosophy and literature is a product of the University: it was with the invention of the University that the wish to separate these things came into being. But if you take away the University judgement on the matter, the classification is absurd. Furthermore, it should *not* be said that in France philosophy is primarily literary: if you take for example the books which I have published, they raise matters of science, and also mathematics. I've done studies of mathematics in antiquity: seventeenth-century mathematics, modern mathematics, nineteenth-century physics, virtually the whole range of the history of science. I've been an historian of science; the history of science, epistemology, is an old French tradition.

The only thing in which France is somewhat behind is the discipline we call logic, and that is simply because of the war, in which the greatest logicians perished; several logicians died in the 1914 war, and others died in the 1939 war. But, apart from that, French philosophy has always had an encyclopaedic scope. The real French tradition which carries on, and which I hope myself to carry on, is that of Descartes, Auguste Comte, Diderot and of Bergson himself, for whom philosophy must have an encyclopaedic base. That is, the philosopher must be a person who knows mathematics, physics, chemistry, biology and so on, just as in the approach of August Comte.

RM: By encyclopaedic you don't mean the tendency to collect up all the factual items possible . . .

MS: No, no, not at all . . .

RM: In order to get a complete picture.

MS: This complete picture must be forgotten before philosophy is undertaken, a bit like the Marquise of the eighteenth century who said that the principles of good manners had to be learnt in order to be forgotten as soon as possible. Otherwise, people would in the end be still less polite than they were normally. I think this is an old French tradition, and in this respect I consider that I try to be, and to work, according to this tradition. I've written on mathematics, physics, biology, on the humanities . . .

RM: And literature.

MS: Yes, and literature is part of the grounding, you see, and that's what the French tradition is: it's a certain relationship to knowledge which does not hold that philosophy is a specialism such as metaphysics, logic or linguistics. It's a kind of globalization.

RM: Yes: I think that the very word discipline contains this notion of division, of something cut off.

MS: That's right. For example, you yourself discuss the history of religions: I am extremely attentive to developments in that field. I have done a lot of work on people like Dumézil, and other more recent theorists, and for me the history of religion is also part of this philosophical groundwork. I can't imagine philosophy as a discipline. I think that philosophy is a sum, a sum . . .

RM: A *summa*.

MS: In the sense of a *summa*, yes.

RM: So you are interested in comparative religion. Are you interested in Eliade, for example?

MS: Yes, I have read almost everything he has written: I was trained in history of religions within the triangle Georges Dumézil, Mircea Eliade and René Girard. But of course a philosopher doesn't go into the fine details of the history of religions, but looks at what is happening in the theory which goes with it.

RM: So you're a specialist in the thought of Leibniz . . .

MS: I was, I was . . .

RM: You're no longer one?

MS: No, no. There's a vulgar expression in French, 'I've already given'. When they pass around the plate at church it's what you say when you don't give, because you've already given once: it's a common expression. When I wrote my Leibniz I was an historian of philosophy, a competent specialist in the field, I did my thesis, and, as far as this field is concerned, 'I've already given'. And I wanted passionately to get out of it. I think that you have to be a specialist, but afterwards you have to move away from your specific field. I wrote the book on Leibniz because at the beginning of my career I was a mathematician, and I lived through the great revolution which saw modern mathematics put forward in opposition to classical mathematics. When I was a student, we changed mathematics, and it was a bit like changing one's language. This revolution was of great interest to me, and it was partly the reason for my becoming a philosopher. In studying the history of philosophy, I saw Leibniz as both a classical mathematician and a modern mathematician: he was classical in the sense that he was a follower of the dynamics school, a theoretician of calculus and so on, but otherwise he had an extraordinarily contemporary concept of algebra, geometry and topology. So I studied Leibniz because I felt that he anticipated this revolution in mathematics – there was a kind of equilibrium between the old form of mathematics and the new one. We moved from a mathematics of function to that of *structure*. In large part, what was called structuralism in France was in my view invalidated because people looked for this idea of structure in linguistics, whereas it was very well-defined in algebra. The extent to which I followed, and even anticipated, the structuralist revolution, lay in the fact that I had myself studied structure in the algebraic sense within modern mathematics. So my work on Leibniz was at once that of a classical historian and that of a 'structuralist', insofar as Leibniz anticipated modern structuralism.

RM: And Leibniz is also interested in Christianity.

MS: Yes, there is a theology in Leibniz. I discuss it several times in my book, but several years later I wrote a preface to a translation of the letters of Leibniz to Father Des Bosses, which belongs to the latter part of Leibniz' life. Here, it seems that Leibniz moved from a traditional theology . . . to a Christian theology . . . and I was very impressed by this translation because I felt that here Leibniz had added, in a sense, to his system a kind of meditation on Christianity.

RM: Can we move now to your *Hermes*, the five books of which a selection has been published in English under the same title. The title is interesting: in antiquity Hermes was associated with hermeneutics, and he was the ambassador of logos, of reason. What did you mean by the title?

MS: It had a very precise meaning. You would know that there were in a way two Hermes. Of course it is true that in many ways Hermes symbolizes the god of hermeneutics, in that he has a bit of an Egyptian background, with Hermes Trismegistus, but it is not entirely that aspect which I had in mind for the title of my books. I was rather thinking of the more classical god, Hermes, of communication, the god of transport, commerce, of sailors – the god whose statue was placed at the crossroads of various towns. The Hermes which was mutilated, they say, by Alcibiades.

RM: That's the Hermes of classical Greece.

MS: Yes, it is the Hermes of classical Greece who figures in the title of my book. Why? Because, at the end of the war, Marxism held great sway in France, and in Europe. And Marxism taught that the essential, the fundamental infrastructure was the economy and production: I myself thought, from 1955 or 1960 onwards, that production was not important in our society, or that it was becoming much less so, but that what was important was communication, and that we were reaching a culture, or society, in which communication would hold precedence over production.

RM: And what do you understand by 'communication'?

MS: The group of technologies which have now passed into everyday life, which range from telephone communications, for example, to data processing and computers. That technology has in my view meant far more in the modern world than the production of primary materials. And in fact the future quickly showed that I was right, in that coal, steel, and all kinds of industry have more or less disappeared, whereas communication became the very foundation of our society. And I take a little personal pride in the fact that I anticipated in the years 1955 to 1960 the world in which we now live. And at that stage, when I was finishing Leibniz and when I was writing the Hermes series, I was halfway between a structuralism of a mathematical or algebraic kind, and a philosophy of communication, symbolized by Hermes in classical Greece.

I have never been of the linguistic school, or the hermeneutic: I have spent a lot of my life expounding texts, as we do in the university world, but I have never drawn from it a philosophy, as one does within the hermeneutic tradition. My Hermes, my personal one, is the Hermes of communication, of the crossroads. And in a way the reason for my work on Leibniz lay also in the fact that he was the first western philosopher to have established a philosophy which he himself called a philosophy of the communication of substances. He calls monadology a philosophy of the communication of substances. So there was a connection between Leibniz and my Hermes.

RM: Communication in Leibniz' sense means a kind of relation?

MS: Yes, exactly. Leibniz is the first to have seen that it was difficult to develop a philosophy of primary particles, or of the atoms, or of the metaphysical atoms, without tracing the paths between the elements, or the relations between the atoms. And he was the first – not the first, because the ancient Stoics had the idea of a universe bound together by series – but he was the metaphysician of the Stoic series.

RM: The idea of relation was not very much developed in ancient philosophy.

MS: No, not even in the classical period. It was Leibniz who really developed this. But with the Stoics there is a genuine idea of the interrelationships between things. Leibniz made of it an idea which was both metaphysical and mathematical, and in this respect he anticipates modern thinking.

RM: In Plato there is practically no notion of relation: there is the same and the other, difference and identity. And difference is a problem: there is nothing to explain the communication between things.

MS: Yes. At the stage when I wrote my Leibniz and my Hermes books, the problem of communication, and the problem of algebraic structures, were pretty much my cup of tea.

RM: May I turn now to a question which we have already touched on, in relation to the language of philosophy. It sometimes seems, particularly in the Anglo-American tradition, to be the goal of philosophy to develop a single rational language, an apodeictic language. Is the goal of philosophical enquiry, in your view, to develop a kind of clean language, rigorous and universal: a sort of computer language?

MS: I don't think that's the goal of philosophy. I am not of the Anglo-American school and I am not a philosopher of language. Consequently, an idea like this has never been central to my concerns, and that for two reasons. Firstly, I was myself a scientist originally: I was a mathematician for many years. And I have often dealt with physics, thermodynamics, questions of biology and so on. For me the language of truth, the language of exactitude and rigour, is the language of science and it has already been found. So why have another language to reach goals which have already been in some sense attained? We already have rigour in mathematics, exactitude in the natural sciences, and so on. Secondly,

I have been very interested in the history of science and I have observed for a long time that there are two mathematical traditions, and not just one. Before the Greeks there was an Egyptian mathematics, or Assyrio-Babylonian, and it's of the algorithmic type. The algorithmic approach is one, and it is this that computer language is rediscovering. It's a very old tradition. And these machine algorithms are of great interest, and they allow a certain type of discovery, of a certain type of truth. But that is one field, and in my view philosophy is entirely different.

RM: You've recently brought out a book, *The Five Senses*, which won the *Prix Médicis* in Paris. What was your motivation in writing this book?

MS: For fifty years, the only question has been the question of language, whether one belongs to the German school, the Anglo-American school or even the French. All you hear about is the spoken language or writing. And in France, Sartre produces *Words*, Foucault writes *Words and Things*, in which language is the chief issue. Recently, a book has come out called *The Grammar of Objects*. In my day little children were given lessons on naming things: it's as if we can only feel or perceive to the extent that we possess language. My book is a reaction against this theory: it can be put clearly in just a few words. We never say 'the colour of the sky' or 'the colour of blood', or 'the colour of wheat', or 'the colour of plums'. We say 'blue', 'red', 'yellow', or 'violet'. So we have words for colours, and there analytic philosophy is right. It is possible in fact that we cannot perceive a variety of blue for which we do not have a name. But it gets more complicated with the sense of smell, and I've been greatly interested in taste and smell, as a Frenchman who likes wine and who can appreciate good wine. You know that the mouth is an organ which is quite . . . weak . . . whereas the sense of taste is an organ of great wealth. In the book I point out that we never say anything other than 'the smell of a rose', or 'the smell of an apricot', or 'the smell of . . . '. We refer to a thing, but there is no name for the smell. And if what the linguistic analysts said were true, we would have no noses, since we have no names for the sensations provided by the sense of smell. There are no adjectives for it. The sense of smell is entirely without adjectives. If analytic philosophy were right, we would be condemned to being without this sense. The linguistic school is a school with no sense of smell, and no taste. Now, when referring to humankind, we say *homo sapiens*, as you know. But people who don't know Latin don't know that *sapiens* refers to tasting with the mouth and the tongue – 'sapidity' comes from that. So we say *homo sapiens* to refer to our species, forgetting that this expression refers primarily to tasting with the mouth, with an organ. The origins of the idea are very important.

RM: That's interesting: in antiquity, man was defined as an animal which laughs. But you say . . .

MS: Yes, I remember: no, I don't say that; I say merely that when we say *homo sapiens*, we've forgotten that the origin of the notion of wisdom, or of discourse – because for us man is speaking man – lies in the capacity to taste with the mouth, and with the sense of smell. For most philosophers this wisdom, this sapience, resides in language.

RM: Taking up an earlier remark, what you say on the language of the sense of smell, or the lack of it, explains perhaps the language of wine and of wine appreciation, in the sense that it's a language which is drawn from other areas; it can be practically incomprehensible.

MS: One chapter of my book, which is called 'Table', is devoted to the description of a glass of white wine, a Bordeaux, which is called Château d'Yquem. I give the year, and I go over the type of language which is required if you're going to give a description of this wine. I try to describe the sensation in order to show how defective language is in the case of this sensation.

RM: Which amounts to saying that there is a human capacity which does not have a language.

MS: This is true of the sense of smell, which is an example I don't in fact give in my book, but which I often give to describe my view: we don't always have the vocabulary for our sensations. I chose there the sense of smell, but there's another example: the varieties of pink distinguished by the painter Van Dyck in the hip of Eve – the number of shades – defies the vocabulary available. Vocabulary is less rich than the varieties of pink used by Van Dyck. So my book is devoted to a defence of the qualitative, the empirical, to a defence of the non-reducibility of the empirical to the logical. I would go so far as to say that a form of knowledge has been lost, an empirical form, blotted out by the linguistic and virtually algebraic revolution.

RM: And are there other developments of this idea? Do you limit it to sensation?

MS: Well I called the book 'The Five Senses', and I discuss of course the sixth sense, this sense we have of our own bodies; there's a whole chapter on the sense of body. This is a new book for me since I have in the past been concerned with scientific questions of the sort we were discussing a moment ago, and the book represents an attempt to reconstruct philosophy in another terrain . . . another terrain, not the one we've been using for the last half-century, which is that of language.

RM: I've been wondering if there's a possible metaphysical extension of these ideas: I was thinking of Wittgenstein's unspeakable, for example.

MS: Perhaps, but the extension is in the subtitle. *The Five Senses* also has the title 'Philosophy of Mixed Bodies': it's the first volume, and after this I'll discuss several other problems, but not within the category of the unspeakable. It's a category which is too easy: it's nothing more than the other side of the speakable. I'm going to organize the remainder under the heading of the idea of mixture, which is a notion which was studied by Plato in the *Philebus*, and then by the Stoics.

RM: Could you explain the meaning of the subtitle: 'Philosophy of Mixed Bodies'? It's the idea of mixture, contact . . .

MS: It is the idea of mixture that I'm going to deal with. What happens when two bodies are so close they cannot be distinguished? I was brought to this question by the question of sensation. I must say, if only for the joke, how amusing it appears to the man in the street that a book on sensation, and there are now dozens of them in English and French, should have to begin by the statement of different algebraic rules. I've never felt the need for algebraic structures, even though this has been my field, to taste a glass of white wine. There's a sort of schizophrenia here, which seems to me to be both laughable and a bit tragic. In the modern world, it must be said, we are indeed losing our senses.

RM: I see a passage on silence in *The Five Senses*. What is the function of silence?

MS: I mention silence in the common or garden sense, and I argue that in our world it no longer exists. It no longer exists because in the open spaces of the country or the sea, where silence once reigned, motors and the media have filled it with noise. We have to fight against the power of noise, which is immense and frightening.

RM: But what we sometimes call silence is in fact a set of noises which we find pleasant or comforting, but absolute silence is something different . . .

MS: I sometimes encountered absolute silence in my youth in the Sahara, or far out to sea with zero wind and a totally calm sea – that is silence in relation to noise. There's another silence which is in relation to language, and again there is a kind of meditation beyond language. In the same manner as the issue of sensation a moment ago, it's self-evident, without having to be argued out, that silence is a precondition of philosophical reflection. Linguistic philosophy overlooks this to the extent that thinking, in this perspective, is the same as speaking. Thinking in my view is first and foremost being silent. It's a necessary condition for the emergence of something else. So it's true that in my books, and in the ones which are to follow, there is much in honour of silence, as opposed to the word.

RM: Yes, in a sense language is made of silence. There have to be silences between words, between syllables. It's distinction, or difference, which allows for language. But you have also in *The Five Senses* a passage on play; the play is situated in the body, and you seem to suggest that there is no play which is specifically distinct from the body, but that there is a type of continuity.

MS: Yes: I said before that there were several passages in the book on the sixth sense, the sensation of one's own body, and in fact I thought I'd amuse myself by carrying out a meditation in the manner of Descartes, but outside all language, and without any reference to an abstract soul; it was a virtual recounting of the birth event. I was able to experience, in a rather tragic circumstance, and I attempt to suggest it here, that the body carries within itself a type of centre, which you could call the subject. It's an analysis which has significance for the understanding of the body, I think.

RM: You're relating the subject to the body: often it's said that Plotinus was the first to formulate the notion of the subject:

he asks the question 'what is the we?', the *hemeis*, several times.

MS: I've said a great deal about the 'we' in a book which came out before *The Five Senses* and which deals with Rome. It's called *Rome: The Book of Foundations*, and in it I analyse the first book of Livy, and the manner in which Roman society established itself. I've attempted to deal with this question: what is the multiplicity, what is the fundamental characteristic of this multiplicity which we can call 'we'?

RM: In the modern world we often make use of the notion of a sole and individual self, isolated, cut off from others – in fact the opposite of the experience of antiquity.

MS: Yes, and in fact it's the opposite of our own experience as well. It's clear as soon as we're in the circle of Hermes that this metaphysical vision of isolated atomic individuals is an abstraction which has nothing to do with reality.

RM: In your book *The Parasite*, which has appeared in English, I think you raise some of these issues.

MS: Yes, I was trying to find a link between elements, between individuals, of an almost atomic character. The relationship between two people, the father/son relationship for example, I called the double-arrow relationship because there are two poles. But the parasitic relationship is a simpler one: it's a single arrow which goes in one direction but not the other, because the parasite is a creature which feeds on another, but gives nothing in return. There's no exchange, no balance sheet to be drawn up; there's no reciprocity in the relationship, which is one-dimensional.

RM: And the parasite grows bigger more quickly than its host.

MS: Yes, there *is* a reciprocity which is difficult to grasp: if the parasite eats too much, he'll kill his host, and it'll die by the same token. And the term 'parasite' has three meanings in French, not two as in English. The parasite in French is firstly someone who eats at the table of another, without being invited: that's the parasite of the Latin and Greek comedies. Then there's the sense drawn from parasitology, the parasite which can even be a microbe, from the single cell creature to the insect, and which feeds on a host. The third meaning, which was used in English a bit at the end of the nineteenth century, is that of static on the line, that is, noise within communication. I've tried to find the coherence between the biological, the sociological and the physical meaning of the parasite.

RM: You really think there's some common thread between the three of them?

MS: Yes, there is one. What I found of interest here was what I call the atom of communication. The simplest link between two things is the parasitic relationship, and this idea provides an analysis which is deeper, more fundamental, than the current analysis of gifts, exchange, and so on, which are always relationships of balance. By contrast, the parasitic relationship is an unbalanced one, particularly in the social sense: when a parasite is your guest in the social sense, there is sometimes some return on the relationship, but the parasite always makes his return in words. One gives him food, but in return he makes fine speeches. There is the beginning of an exchange here, which gives language its correct value: language is the counterfeit money with which food is paid for. This is a very interesting theme in Roman comedy, and it can tell us something about language, and about the philosophy of language *ipso facto*. This was very interesting to me at the time because it was my point of entry into the humanities, coming from the exact sciences, and it was to study the fundamental social relationship, which I consider to be a parasitic one.

RM: And now you occupy a chair of history, is that correct?

MS: History of science: that's my trade; at the outset I was almost exclusively an historian of mathematics. Then I worked on the history of thermodynamics, nineteenth-century physics, and now my field is the history of ideas and history.

RM: And so what do you think of the disciplines, the disciplinary divisions in the university world?

MS: I think that the dividing up of the disciplines into very narrow cells is certainly one of the causes of the effectiveness of science. But from the point of view of truth in general we've lost a lot, and the goal of philosophy should be to try to create a synthesis, where analysis goes off into detail. I've dealt with this at length in two books, in the second volume of *Hermès* which is subtitled 'Interference', and in *Hermès V*, subtitled 'The North–West Passage', and in the latter in particular I examined what is now called interdisciplinary studies.

RM: So philosophy's not a discipline which is set apart, in its own corner.

MS: I called the book 'The North–West Passage' – you know the passage between the Atlantic Ocean and the Pacific, to the north of Canada, which is very difficult and complicated to negotiate – as an image for the passage between the humanities and the exact sciences. I think the job of philosophy is to open up this passage between the exact sciences and the humanities.

RM: To create communication?

MS: Yes: when Socrates was questioned on philosophy in Xenophon's *Symposium*, he replied that it was *mastropeia*; this is a trade of low repute in our society. It is the activity of the person who puts into communication men and women. Philosophy has the job of federating, of bringing things together. So analysis might be valuable, with its clarity, rigour, precision and so on, but philosophy really has the opposite function, a federating and synthesizing function. I think that the foundation of philosophy is the encyclopaedic, and its goal is synthesis.

RM: And does contemporary French philosophy conform to this definition in your view?

MS: Yes, it has always done so, since the eighteenth century. It was encyclopaedic in character then; it endeavoured to bring people together into one *salon*. Experts from all sorts of horizons were brought together into one *salon*. The university functions in the opposite way, in that it divides the experts. I don't know if all French philosophy today conforms to this ideal, but my work does: it doesn't involve a system of thought, but a synthesis.

As I get older I am more and more attracted by ordinary language, a philosophy which does not need terms other than those drawn from everyday language to express itself. I don't think we have to be either grammarians or specialists: I believe in ordinary language. In *The Five Senses* I do not think I've used the word 'transcendental' more than twice. I use technical vocabulary as little as possible now.

RM: Like Plato.

MS: Yes, I think Plato's a leader in that; with him there's an analytic philosopher called Socrates, and a non-analytic philosopher called Plato. There are two of them: Socrates is the grammarian who speaks in short sentences, who analyses, who cuts up into pieces, and who clarifies. He brings clarity, but Plato speaks at length; he writes the *Symposium*, the *Phaedrus* and so on. He's the inspired one, and I believe in this coupling of the grammarian and the stylist, the philosopher and the writer, the scientific intelligence and the literary intelligence. I believe in both.

RM: And you think that ordinary language has more value than we realize?

MS: Not only does it have more value, but it is also true Plato was a great philosopher *because* he expressed magnificently the language of the Athenians. And we have that role too: philosophers have to strive continually to bring ordinary language back to life.

SELECT BIBLIOGRAPHY

Le Système de Leibniz et ses modèles mathématiques, 2 vols, republished in one volume (Paris: Presses Universitaires de France 1982).

Hermès I. La communication (Paris: Minuit 1969).

Hermès II. L'interférence (Paris: Minuit 1972).

Hermès III. La traduction (Paris: Minuit 1974).

Hermès IV. La distribution (Paris: Minuit 1977).

Hermès V. Le passage du Nord–Ouest (Paris: Minuit 1980).

English version in résumé: *Hermes. Literature, Science and Philosophy* (Baltimore: Johns Hopkins University Press 1982).

Feux et signaux de brume. Zola (Paris: Grasset 1975).

La Naissance de la physique dans le texte de Lucrèce. Fleuves et turbulences (Paris: Minuit 1977).

Le Parasite (Paris: Grasset 1980); English version: *The Parasite* (Baltimore: Johns Hopkins University Press 1982).

Rome. Le livre des fondations (Paris: Grasset 1983).

Les Cinq Sens (Paris: Seuil 1986); English version to appear (New York: A. Knopf).

Luce Irigaray is a French national, born in Belgium in 1930. Her initial training was undertaken at Louvain, and her earlier work was on Paul Valéry. She then moved into psychology, linguistics and psychoanalysis. The book Speculum *formed the substance of her Doctorate of Letters thesis, at the University of Paris VIII.*

She is a now Director of Research in Philosophy at the National Centre for Scientific Research, Paris. Her network goes far beyond the academic, and her influence in the field of ideas is very widespread, in academic circles, among feminists, and among the thinking public in general. She is a frequent visitor to Italy, and contributes regularly to the newspaper of the Italian Communist Party. Luce Irigaray's recent work takes her to the forefront of psycho-linguistic enquiry, particularly in the area of gender in language.

4

LUCE IRIGARAY

Luce Irigaray consented to this interview only on the basis that questions were provided in writing. This was done: the questions turned on the issue of sexuality in discourse; on Mme Irigaray's claim to have identified the characteristics of female discourse; and her view that language is never neuter (*neutre*). After some discussion over a *bouillabaisse* in a Paris restaurant, she sent the following statement.

You wrote saying that you would like to have my thoughts on two specific themes: why is the sexualization of discourse one of the most significant questions of our time? And how can this be translated into a language such as the French language, for example? I'll reply to both questions simultaneously, moving from one to the other.

Why is the sexualization of discourse one of the major questions of our time? Humanity today needs the difference between the sexes in order to regenerate itself and to continue to develop. Freud put forward a number of highly debatable ideas on sexual difference, but he did state that the sexes regenerate each other quite apart from the procreation process. He also confessed his incompetence in the area of female sexuality. It is crucial that we rethink, following Freud, the transition from nature to culture, as it concerns sexual difference – and following Marx as well. There is a question of cultural truth on the nature/culture relation, and there is also a question of social justice. Sexual difference is a matter of the relationship between women and men, and not only between the son and his mother, as is held in one of the most resilient traditions in our culture. It is probably the reduction of the difference between the

63

sexes to this issue which explains why the question of gender in language has scarcely been raised up until now, and why it encounters such resistance. The signs for the plural, for example, can remain in the masculine provided that male relations only are involved, and this indicates that exchanges on the public level are exclusively masculine exchanges. The linguistic code, like the modes of exchange, like the system of images, and representation, is made for masculine subjects. Thus God is father; he begets a son, and for this purpose he uses a woman who is reduced to maternity. This has been the most abiding structure in our religious and civic traditions for centuries: a relation *between* men, or *in* man . . . through a woman. In such a culture the woman remains at home, and is the object of use and exchange between men. She is used for reproduction and for the material maintenance of life: since culture is a culture between men, there is nothing wrong, linguistically speaking, in saying Mr X and Mr Y met for an exchange of views on politics, or cultural matters, or commercial matters. Language is coded on the basis of social realities, of real facts. We see today how it continues to develop with the inclusion of certain words in the dictionary. Sexism, for example, but not only . . . there are also foreign words, words drawn from technology, and so on. Things get complicated apparently, on the level of grammar: the human race tends to be of the view that the rules of syntax are eternal and unchangeable. This is part of a fear of social change. As Nietzsche says, we will always believe in God while we believe in grammar.

It is indeed the same set of beliefs. The God of men requires the maintenance of grammatical rules; the God of women, or their divinities, singular or plural, requires change in the linguistic code. Why? Because God or Goddess, in the singular or the plural, corresponds to a collective phenomenon; no God the father, without the race of men, no Goddess, without the race of women. The entry of women into the public world, the relations between them and men, necessitate today a number of social changes, and changes in language in particular. If Monsieur the President of the Republic meets Madame the Queen, you say they met: '*ils se sont rencontrés*', which is close to a grammatical anomaly. Instead of dealing with this delicate question, most people wonder whether we must be governed either by men alone, or by women alone, which means by one single gender. The weight of the rules of language can lead to such impasses. Unfortunately that which is at stake is not yet perceived in its reality, and, if the race of men resists this evolution in the rules of grammar, some women, even feminists (not all, fortunately) are willing to say that the masculine gender will be adequate for them if they may use it.

Neutralizing grammatical gender is equivalent to the annulment of the difference in sexual subjectivity, and it tends increasingly to exclude sexuality from culture. We will take a big step backwards if we abolish grammatical gender, a step backwards which our culture cannot afford. On the other hand, it is urgent and indeed imperative that equal subjective rights be given to men and women; 'equal' meaning, of course, different. 'Subjective' implies rights which are equivalent in modes of exchange. From the linguistic point of view this means examining the cultural injustices perpetrated by language, without any systematic sexism. This is signalled in grammar; it's signalled in the connotations of words. For centuries, that which is considered to be of value has been of the masculine gender; what has been devalued is of the feminine gender. The sun, for example, *le soleil*, is masculine; the moon, *la lune*, is feminine. The sun is considered in our cultures to be the source of life; but the moon is seen as ambiguous, virtually sinister. The attribution of the masculine gender to the sun can be found throughout the history of human culture: the link between the sun and the god-man as well. This tradition does not constitute an immutable truth; it evolves over a long period, and there are different speeds of development in different cultures and within different languages. The positive connotation of the masculine gender, the gender of words, is tied to the impact of the establishment of the patriarchy, and in particular to the appropriation of divinity by men. This is not a minor question. It is a very important one. Without divine power, men would not have been able to supplant the relationship between mother and daughter, and its consequences in nature and society. But man becomes God by giving himself an invisible father, a father tongue. Man becomes God as Word, and as Word made flesh. Sperm, whose power in the procreation process is not immediately visible, is relayed through the linguistic code, the logos. This linguistic code tries to become the all-embracing truth. There are, in the appropriation of language by men, at least three manoeuvres: first, the attempt to prove that they are fathers; secondly the attempt to prove that they are more powerful than mothers; thirdly, the attempt to prove that they can engender the horizons of culture as they themselves have engendered within the sphere of nature, in insemination, within the belly of a woman. To be sure that he will not be betrayed in his power, the race of man represents voluntarily, or involuntarily, that which is of value as corresponding to his image and his grammatical gender. Most linguists will say that grammatical gender is arbitrary, neutral, and independent of sexual gender: this is incorrect. They haven't thought it through. The question has not been a crucial one for them: their personal subjectivity, their theory, and so on, has made itself comfortable in the high value placed on being masculine, passing itself off as neuter, arbitrary and universal. Patient work on the gender of words reveals their hidden sex: this is not expressed immediately, and a linguist will quickly object that a lounge chair, *un fauteuil*, is no more masculine than an ordinary chair, *une chaise*. Apparently not, but a little thought shows that the the lounge chair is more valuable than the ordinary chair. The chair, the feminine one, is simply more useful, and the masculine is more luxurious, ornamental, culturally signalled. A rigorous analysis of all the words in the dictionary will bring out their hidden sex; the computer, *l'ordinateur*, is of course masculine, whereas the typewriter, *la machine à écrire*, is feminine. It's a question of value. It has to be the masculine, which prevails: the plane, *l'avion*, is superior to the car, *la voiture*; the Boeing, *le Boeing*, is greater than the Caravelle, and so on. How did the gender of words come about? There are different levels of attribution: at the most archaic level, I think that there is an identification of the reality designated, and of the sex of the speaker. The sun *is* man, the god-man. The moon *is* woman, the sister of the god-man. The earth *is* woman, the sky *is* her brother, a man, and so on. There is still something which remains of this identification in the gender of words, which can be more or less explicit, or more or less concealed. But there is another factor apart from the identification between the word and its designated reality. Living beings, animated beings, cultivated beings, become part of the masculine. Objects which are inanimate, deprived of life, inhuman, turn out to be feminine. This means that men have attributed to themselves subjectivity, and have reduced women to the status of objects. This is true for women themselves, but it's also true for the gender of words. Thus the harvester is a man, but if, in terms of the present debate over the names of the professions, the linguist and those who make rules want to call the woman-harvester a harvesteress, the word is unavailable for the woman subject; the harvesteress is in fact a useful tool for the harvester. There is therefore no place for the sexual human couple. Men are surrounded by women/objects, and by feminine tools. They do not create the world on equal terms with women, as sexual subjects. This can only become possible by a mutation of language. But this mutation can only be carried out through a re-enhancing of the value of the femine gender. The feminine gender, which was originally different, is more or less assimilated today with the masculine nouns: being woman means not being a man.

This is what psychoanalysis calmly asserts, in theory and practice, with its view about penis envy, or the desire for the phallus. This reality belongs simply to a certain stage of culture and a certain state of the language. In this context the liberation of women does not consist in becoming male, or the desire for male parts or objects of men, but in the revaluing of the expression of their sex as feminine subjects. This is quite different. The misunderstanding over the acquisition of equality and liberation through the possession of objects, or through access to a subjectivity of the same value, is maintained by various practices and social theories. Psychoanalysis for example, but Marxism as well. These theories are developed by men, and in the German language: they have had in recent times great success in Anglo-Saxon countries, because these cultures place the sign of the woman's gender on the object. In these countries a woman can have *her* child, whereas in French she has *his* child, *son enfant*, whether it's a boy or a girl. She can have *her* penis and *her* phallus. This is not possible in the Romance languages. Thus Anglo-Saxon women can claim equality through the possession of objects together with the signs of their gender; having acquired this, they abandon in the end the right to the sign of gender on the subjective level. This fact continues to cause misunderstandings in the so-called women's liberation movement. For many an Anglo-Saxon feminist it is enough to have *her* university job, to have written *her* book, to be liberated. For me, and this is becoming more and more deliberate among women of the Romance language countries, the goal is to become a free feminine subject. For this liberation language is a tool, a productive tool like any other one. I must develop it to obtain subjective rights equivalent to those of men, in order to exchange language and objects with them. In one case, the liberation of women highlights the equality of objective rights, the difference between men and women is situated in the nature, the quantity and sometimes the quality of objects conquered, or possessed. In the other, sexual liberation means reaching a subjective status, socially and individually, as woman. The emphasis is on the difference between the rights of the masculine and feminine subjects. Possessing objects which are equivalent to those of men does not resolve the question of gender for women of the Romance languages, because such objects do not at present bear the signs of their subjective owners. We say *mon enfant* whether we're men or women. So, for objects of value, the sign of possession is identical: as for other objects, these are generally devalued when they are used or appropriated by women.

The problem of the object and its conquest cannot therefore resolve the problem of sexual inequality in all languages. I think that it can't be resolved in any language. But some requirements, some urgent problems can be met. If the issue of the names of the professions seems so important, it's because it occupies an intermediary position between subject and object. Thus one *possesses* a professional status, one *has* a job, and money, but these things are not possessable like any old object. They are part of the subjective identity although they are not by themselves sufficient to constitute it. Further, this demand is easily linked to social demands which are already present in the masculine world. The issue can be put simply: *he* receives general support, he only sees in opposition to himself realities which are already encoded linguistically, harvesteress, *cafetière* (coffee-maker), and so on, and social resistance according to the level of social access allowed or prohibited to women. This involves linguistic anomalies which are quite amusing: I'll give you an example.

This example comes from a column published in the newspaper *L'indépendant* for the third of September 1987. It concerns the death of Nicole Chouraqui:

Paris. Nicole Chouraqui, ancien secrétaire-général adjoint du RPR, est décédée à son domicile parisien à l'âge de quarante-neuf ans des suites d'un cancer. Née à Alger le 18 mars 1938, cette économiste de formation, après une carrière d'analyste financier à la Banque de L'Union Parisienne de 1960 à 1966, s'était engagée dans la vie politique en adhérant au Parti Radical. En 1970 elle rejoint le RPR dont elle sera membre du bureau politique jusqu'à 1977, puis secrétaire-général adjoint en 1978, secrétaire national chargée du travail de 1981–1984: elle est élue député européen en 1979, et réélue en 1984. Conseiller de Paris dans le 19e arrondissement, adjoint au maire Jacques Chirac, elle était aussi conseiller régional, Ile de France, mariée à l'assureur Claude Chouraqui; elle était mère de deux filles.

Paris. Nicole Chouraqui, former deputy general-secretary of the RPR, Member of the European Parliament, Deputy Mayor of Paris, died of cancer at her Paris home at the age of 49. She was born at Algiers on the 18th of March 1938, and was an economist by training; after a career as a financial analyst, at the Parisian Union Bank from 1960–1966, she entered political life by joining the Radical Party. In 1970 she joined the RPR, and was a member of the political committee until 1977, and then deputy general-secretary in 1978, national secretary responsible for the period from 1981–1984: she was elected a member of the European Parliament in 1979, and was re-elected in 1984. She was councillor for the 19th district of Paris and assistant to the Mayor Jacques Chirac; she was also the regional councillor for the Ile de France. She was married to Claude Chouraqui, of the insurance industry, and was the mother of two daughters.

This example is about the announcement of the death of a woman politician. I think it's significant. In order for it to be possible to talk about this woman by herself, it was perhaps necessary that she should die. Who knows? In this little article, everything which is to do with the identity allowed to a woman, is in the feminine. The rest is in the masculine. So Nicole Chouraqui indeed died, with the feminine e, *décédée*, at her home at the age of 49. She was indeed born (*née* with an e) in Algiers, on the 18th of March 1938; she was indeed married, *mariée* with an e, to Claude Chouraqui of the insurance industry. And she was the mother of two daughters. Bravo for the daughters, and not 'children'. Our culture is indeed making progress. But the remainder of the little article has a number of grammatical anomalies. Shifts in the use of gender show that we're in a period of a change in this regard. For example: Nicole Chouraqui is the former deputy general-secretary of the RPR, in the masculine, *ancien secrétaire-général adjoint* of the RPR, and not in the feminine, *ancienne secrétaire-générale adjointe* of the RPR. Is it because she herself, or the RPR, had a female assistant secretary, or a stenographer/typist, or computer operator, herself undoubtedly of the feminine gender? Or is it because the job of deputy general-secretary of the RPR is virtually always held by a man, and that it would be almost sacrilegious to feminize the name of such a high profession? These two alternatives are linked to the question about the difference in value attributed to the masculine and feminine genders. Continuing with this article, I see that Nicole Chouraqui was a member of the European Parliament, *député européen* in the masculine, and not *députée européene*. *Député* is in fact a past participle made into a noun; it could quite easily revert to its grammatical category and be put in the feminine. But if it remains a masculine noun, can the adjective which goes with it be put in the feminine, to refer to a woman? Continuing, Nicole Chouraqui is indeed a feminine economist, *cette économiste*, by training; the economist by training can remain in the feminine gender, but by contrast, and I quote: 'after a career as a financial analyst [masculine] at the Parisian Union Bank from 1960 to 1966, she entered [feminine] political life by joining the Radical Party. In 1970 she joined the RPR, and became its deputy general-secretary in 1978.' Here we have again the masculine where there is access to professional life and access to prestigious political posts. Women can therefore pursue, as women, training in economics, but not the career of financial analyst, or of deputy general-secretary of the party. Continuing the quotation: 'national secretary' is the masculine, but *she* can nevertheless be responsible, in the feminine, for the period 1981–1984.

I repeat: 'National secretary, responsible [*chargée*, in the feminine] for the period 1981–1984: *she* was elected a member

of the European Parliament in 1979, and was re-elected in 1984.'
As an academic she can be feminine, but at work the grammatical
agreements have to be reviewed. If Nicole Chouraqui was the
secretary, responsible, *chargée*, in the feminine, why was she not
national secretary in the feminine, for example? To sum up: this
little extract, which undoubtedly aims to be rigorously correct,
provides an amusing demonstration of the present difficulty in
applying the grammatical code as it applies to gender.

This gives us three reasons immediately for concerning
ourselves with grammatical gender: first, we have to rethink
the movement from nature to culture. We have to remember
that the living world is sexual, but that it is composed of two
sexes: culture should therefore express the sexuality of two
living subjects, woman and man. Secondly, it is important
to realize that it is impossible to emerge from social injustice
without reform or revolution in the means of production
and communication which the linguistic codes consist of.
Thirdly, these are in a critical situation today, given the number
of women who have entered the circuit of the schools, the
university and the working world. It is no longer possible
to ignore the fact that such women are valid subjects of
communication, and not just objects for use and exchange
between men. Language must develop, unless the politician or
theoretician wants to use it cynically as a means of repression.
I think rather that they are insensitive to the question and that
they have to be alerted to it. And my last point: it's not only a
problem of discourse. It is useless to blame women once again by
saying that all these inequalities arise from their state or are their
fault. For language only partly allows them to be other than they
are: I'll give a few examples based on the analysis of discourse
recorded in therapy or in experiments.

Among the results obtained I have found it very significant
that, first, women rarely refer to themselves as the subject of a
statement. They leave the place to 'you', the man, or more rarely
a woman, except in a therapeutic situation with a woman. Or to
'he', his ideas and feelings, to the order of the language or of
the world, to concrete objects. Women reflect in their discourse
the social order and the linguistic rules: they express a society
which is between men, its organization, its ideas or convictions,
because they have no social and linguistic order which is
appropriate to them. If women submit so wholeheartedly to the

existing patriarchal order it is because they lack the linguistic codes to mark themselves off from it. To assert that women don't want anything else amounts to saying that someone locked in a prison or abandoned on a desert island doesn't want anything else. These things are said by men but also by women, which is a sign of their blind alienation in the existing symbolic process. Women are committed to two gigantic tasks: assuming consciousness of the order of language and of one's tongue as sexualized, and also of creating a new symbolic morphology in which she can say: I, sexual being, woman, assert such and such, take such and such action and so on. Meanwhile the only activity which endeavours to take women into language is the narrative discourse. *She* tells about herself. That's probably better than being obliged to keep quiet, no doubt, and it also makes it possible to say 'I, woman' and to narrate her personal history. That has cathartic effects which sometimes compete with those provided by psychoanalysis. But it doesn't establish a new framework and code of symbolic exchanges. This position amounts to the traditional place allowed to women: they tell about themselves, just as they embroider, do tapestry or knitting. And it's sometimes more linear and less liberating, since it is the case that the code is not appropriate to them. Telling about oneself, *se raconter*, still does not involve giving oneself an individual and collective subject, a social and personal identity; a sexual life, and a political life; the values of truth, beauty and religion. That women tell about themselves in fact renders service to the established logic: women create little trouble when they tell about themselves. Unless they count on statistical enquiries which tell about them in the second degree, and impose on them a subjective order from the outside. That's a possibility, but it's a very ambiguous one. It is curious that in linguistic tests, women 'say' themselves much less than men. They rather set up strategies for eliminating the 'I', whereas men, who are considered to be objective and scientific, say 'I', and express judgements of value or of passion. For example, for an instruction of the type 'make a sentence with the word celibate', men immediately respond with, and I quote, 'I am against the celibacy of priests'. Or, 'I live in happy celibacy'. Or again, 'I couldn't care less about my celibacy, I'm a psychologist', and so on. These sentences are absent from the responses of women: men regulate the order of the city and of the culture but they are individually much more disordered than women. So, at the level of the explicit subject of the phrase, women leave the place to 'you', in most cases masculine, and to 'he'. Men on the other hand say 'I' or 'he'. Secondly, on the level of the explicit interlocutor, also, women yield to the masculine, except in (psycho) analysis with one or some women, and I'll come back to this. In the majority of sentences in which there is a designated interlocutor, he is designated as man. When the word which designates the interlocutor could refer to a man or a woman, like the word *lui** in French, that is to say when there's an ambiguity over the partners in the discourse, women lift the ambiguity in favour of the 'he', and not in favour of the 'she'. Thus the instruction to form a simple sentence with the words 'problems', 'he'* and 'say', these three words, results with men in a sentence of the type: 'I tell him my problems.' Or, 'I tell him that I have problems', or, 'He tells him that he has problems' ['*Je lui dis*', or '*il lui dit*' in each case]. The subject of the statement is a man, and he speaks to a man. There are therefore two or three men who speak to each other: the subject of the statement, who produces the phrase, and in addition the same person again who says 'I', as well as the person to whom he speaks. In this case that makes two men. Or the subject of the statement talks about a man, talking to another man. That makes three men. There may even be four of them: the subject of the statement talks about a man telling another man about the problems of a fourth man, or the problems he's having with a fourth man. For example he tells him [*il lui dit*] that he, another, has problems with him, that is with another man. Men sexualize their discourse less quickly, but they stick together.

This means a sexual choice is made. Women, for their part, often understand the ambiguous word '*lui*' in the masculine sense. Thus to sentences like 'I tell him that I am bored', or, 'I would like to tell him that he has problems', and to the question, 'Who is he [*lui*]?', women reply, 'my good friend' [*mon camarade*], 'a man', 'my friend' [*mon ami*], 'my husband', 'Peter', and so on. Further, they often form sentences of the type, 'He's going to tell him that he's got a problem.' Or, 'He tells him about his problem.' Or, 'He tells him that he is bored', or, 'He tells him about his boredom with being there', or, 'He

*Translator's note: '*lui*', which used in the dative can be either masculine or feminine.

tells him the irritation he felt at going so far away', and so on. In these sentences, where the subject is masculine, *'lui'* is sometimes released of its ambiguity by being made feminine. I think that this is because, by virtue of the structure of the situation, the woman plays the role of mother-interlocutor, in whom one confides one's problems. There is therefore an extra-linguistic constraint in this case: apart from this constraint the interlocutor is masculine. The fact that society is a society between men, and that the linguistic order reflects this reality, weighs very heavily on the discourse of women. And this has a decisive impact on their identity. Women have as primary interlocutrice their mother, that is a person of the same sex as themselves. To compel them to move to the cultural discourse of the 'he' and the 'between hes' means in the first place that they are deprived of their first affective relationship, and of their first 'you', their first interlocutrice. Further, and at the same time, it has the effect of exiling them from their sexual identity, which is constituted as a feminine process, in relation with a 'you' and 'she' who are feminine. The first relation for a woman is a relation between two women: culture exiles them from this relation of communication, never leaving them alone as between women, and without providing for ways of signifiying the female gender when they are in a heterosexual situation. Even in private life, which is the field allegedly reserved to women, language blots out the identity of women. So one says of a couple, they love each other, *ils s'aiment*, they marry each other, *ils s'épousent*, they live together, but also they are a handsome couple, *beaux*, they are old, *âgés*; all made over into the masculine in French. Movements of sexual liberation have not managed to abolish this subordination of the feminine subject to the masculine subject. And women must stay between themselves, so that the feminine plural gender may become possible. Which, again, almost never happens in society. From this point of view co-education does not help at all, and co-education makes a change to the rules of language an urgent matter. If this does not happen, women will be compelled to hold themselves aloof from the company of men, as happens in certain women's liberation groups. I don't think that these activists have thought much about this factor in their tendency to foster non-mixed association. I think that these women have, that *we* have, because I do go to single-sex meetings, understood the weight of the content of discourse, but not always the form of language. I myself have realized the importance of this only recently, though I have sensed it for a long time. From this come certain strategies for writing which are sometimes difficult to handle, but which are necessary if we want to preserve the feminine identity . . . for example the e of the feminine gender in French in all plurals, or sometimes the publication of lectures addressed to women only, and so on. Thus we can preserve the sign of gender in the plural [*ils/elles*] as well. But we do live in a mixed society, and there is no reason to have recourse to clandestine processes in order to become free subjects. The consciousness of the problem should bring about the possibility of a solution. Unless there is a deliberate desire to maintain one sex as subject to another. I think, I hope, that this is perhaps not the case with most people. But few people are aware, *conscients et conscientes*, with an e, of the scale of the question. To the extent that men are themselves deprived of their first female interlocutrice, the maternal one, and they are without a 'you' who is woman and sexualized, they are by the same token deprived of a certain type of exchange, and this is not conducive to the development of an inter-sexual set of relationships for them. If women lose the possibility of relating to themselves as feminine, of communicating among themselves, men will go round in circles within an auto-erotic framework, within auto-affection, narcissism, transposed on to the level of language, or within relations of seduction or possession amongst themselves. Several examples can be given: the format of the discourse of a male neurotic – and who is not? – can be reduced to a sentence of the type, 'I say to myself that I am perhaps loved', or, 'I wonder if I am loved'. What the woman says comes down to this: 'Do you love me?' In the first case all you have is play, and a relationship with oneself, though with a little doubt, and some indirect questioning. There is only 'you' in female discourse. The feminine is reduced to being a possible object of affects or acts of the 'you'. Psychoanalysis may bring out the fact that this 'you' is originally a woman-mother, but in everyday life this 'you' becomes a masculine 'you'. Freud can tell us what he likes about the rationality of the Oedipus theory, but he does not take account of this linguistic necessity. That the little girl must turn away from her mother, that, in my language at least, must be counted as a learning experience, a rite of passage, in the world of the 'he'. This experience, which has no apprenticeship or love, leaves girls in a state of profound subjective dereliction: they will only get over it, Freud says, by becoming mothers, by enduring the procreation process, the procreation of a boy if possible. 'He' and 'she' will say 'they', *ils* in the masculine, but she will be for some months, or years, the elder of the two, the bigger, the responsible one of the pair. Today we can do better. There are other examples of lack of self-affection in the discourse of women. If you ask women to make a sentence using the reflexive *se*, they put the subject of the phrase in the masculine, *il*. They wash themselves, *ils se lavent*, they see themselves, *ils se voient*, they, *ils*, begin to travel, they, *ils*, buy themselves a car. *He* got up early that morning; he wonders what to do, and so on.

If women do gain some consciousness of the problem, they prefer to use the infinitive or a form which replaces the verb, rather than say: she does something for herself, *elle se* . . . . For example, she looked at herself, *elle se regardait*, is a very rare form of words. An example of the tendency to replace 'she' with a neutral form is found in the following construction: to know oneself is to love oneself. To say to oneself, to talk to oneself, or to keep moving is to live, *se déplacer, c'est vivre*. These sentences I obtained from a seminar which I took this winter in Paris. Even when given the words 'dress', 'oneself', 'see', which tend to produce she as subject, women manage to produce sentences like, and I quote, 'He can't see himself in a dress.' Or, 'A boy would like to see himself in a dress.' Or, 'Those [*ceux*, masculine plural] whom I see in this dress look superb [*beaux*, in the masculine]' and so on. Or a woman makes the dress the subject. Thus: 'The dress can be seen from a distance.' In order to get 'she' as the subject, a whole determined environment is necessary to change the pattern. For example, 'She sees herself in *this* dress.' Or again, 'She sees herself in a dress in the mirror.' Or again, 'She sees herself in a dress.' The sentences of the type, 'She sees herself in a dress', are very rare coming from women. Many other examples could be given. To sum it up now, I would refer you to the journal *Langages*, on sex in language, for March 1987, and to my book *Sexes et Parentés*, published by Minuit in 1987. Here other material on the question of the subjective and the objective expression of gender is provided, by me in *Sexes et Parentés*, and by me and others in 'Le sexe linguistique'.

I'll conclude with a few remarks. In the discourse of women, whatever the extent of their, or our, subjection, some subjective values should be preserved. So, on the basis of my analysis of the data: first, women stress much more relations with the other sex. Men remain with each other. Secondly, women are much more interested in others in general. That's signalled in several syntactic procedures, particularly in the importance of transitive verbs, with animate personal objects. For example: 'I wash *him*', 'I love *him*', and so on. Thirdly, women are much more interested in the issue of place: they are alongside others, alongside things. Which recalls one of the Indo–European roots of the verb 'to be'. Women would make being, silently. Men would say 'I am'. Fourthly, women are much more interested in the qualities of people, of things, of the action taking place. Their discourse contains many more adjectives and adverbs than that of men. This raises a very interesting linguistic problem, about the prior discourse produced by a woman, since the adjective usually constitutes a transformation of previous discourse. Fifthly, women are more interested in the present, or the future, whereas men are interested in the past. Sixthly, women are more attentive in transmitting a message than men. They always make an effort to say something, even in an experimental situation. Men remain inert, unless their message is about the state of their soul.

I do not think that it is necessary to remove these character- istics of feminine discourse: on the contrary, women must be permitted to advocate their values publicly. Will they never- theless lose these qualities? I don't think so. They are part of their sexual identity. The important thing is that they should become free subjects while remaining, or becoming, women, and not in endeavouring to become men. Men today, without valid sexual partners, use an abstract discourse which is repetitive and backward-looking, cut off from the concrete and living environment. They spend their lives trying to be as good as their fathers or brothers without cultivating their bodies or their sexuality. They develop objects which are consumable or exchangeable in a competitive sense, but they don't develop themselves as sexual subjects. A sexual culture has still to be developed. I think that Marx, Freud and the movements of sexual liberation, in particular the women's movement, have opened up questions which should not be recited as truths or dogmas, but which should be pursued and developed. Our civilization needs it.

We cannot afford to allow the vibrations of death to continue to drown out the vibrations of life, if I may use terms which are rather too dichotomized for my taste. Our culture cannot carry on the eternal war between men, between men and nature, failing to make a public and cultural alliance between the world of women and that of men.

SELECT BIBLIOGRAPHY

Spéculum, de l'autre femme (Paris: Minuit 1974); English translation: *Speculum of the Other Woman*, trans. Gillian C. Gill (Ithaca: Cornell University Press 1985).

Ce Sexe qui n'en est pas un (Paris: Minuit 1977); English translation: *This Sex Which is Not One*, trans. Catherine Porter and Carolyn Burke (Ithaca: Cornell University Press 1985).

Amante marine. De Friedrich Nietzsche (Paris: Minuit 1983).

L'Oubli de l'air. Chez Martin Heidegger (Paris: Minuit 1983).

Ethique de la différence sexuelle (Paris: Minuit 1984).

Parler n'est jamais neutre (Paris: Minuit 1985).

Sexes et Parentés (Paris: Minuit 1987).

(ed.) 'Le Sexe linguistique', *Langages* 85, March 1987.

Michèle Le Doeuff was born in 1948, and currently holds a research post in the Centre National de la Recherche Scientifique (Paris). She previously taught at the Ecole Normale Supérieure (Fontenay-aux-Roses). Her work is united by certain thematic lines of enquiry, though it is quite disparate in appearance. The impressive body of her historical work on Francis Bacon, and the history of science, is less well-known in Anglo-Saxon countries than her work on feminism, and the idea of the subject. Outside France she is particularly identified by her work on the philosophic 'imaginary'. Her own exploration of this theme gives her historical writing and her contemporary writing a consistency which turns on certain observations about philosophical method. Some of these observations are gender-based, but all could be described as critical: there is an enquiry into philosophy itself in Le Doeuff's work.

5

MICHÈLE Le DOEUFF

RM: It's not very common for French philosophers to be interested in the British philosophical tradition, yet much of your recent work has been on the thought of Francis Bacon, and you've taken the rare step of crossing the Channel. Could you say what your own training has been like, and how you became interested in the English tradition? Did you do philosophy at school, for example?

ML: Philosophy, as you know, is taught in France during the final year of the *lycée*, that is the high school. And it is an important subject, especially for the pupils or students taking A levels in the humanities. When I was 16, I took philosophy for nine hours a week for one year, in order to prepare for that kind of A level. And just after getting the *agrégation*, which is the national competitive examination for teaching . . .

RM: The *agrégation* is a kind of competition in which only a certain number of people are accepted or 'received'. It is a *concours*: is that correct?

ML: Yes, it is.

RM: Is it a form of recruitment for secondary teaching, or does it lead into university work as well?

ML: Both in a way. If you don't pass the *agrégation* you have very little chance of ever being hired by a university. But the *agrégation* in itself is not enough to be hired by a university.

So after the *agrégation* I taught philosophy in *lycées* for a while and enjoyed it: this may sound exotic, I suppose, to anyone involved in the English tradition. But the kind of philosophy we teach or are taught at that level may sound even more exotic. There is a syllabus listing forty questions for an A level in the humanities (twenty questions for students taking the scientific A level), including issues such as: consciousness, the unconscious, desire, power, society and the state, the other, history, theory and experience, work, liberty, religion, and so forth. Now we think that teenagers *are* able to manage the theories of Aristotle or Marx when we discuss the question of work, or society. We believe they can read a page by Kant when we talk about freedom, or a text by Plato, with our help, of course. And this is a feature of the French way of philosophizing, not to separate philosophical reasoning from knowledge of the history of philosophy, or acquaintance with the classics. Not only at school, but later on, at the university as well. In other words, when we discuss a philosophical problem, art for instance, we do always refer to the Greeks, or Kant or Hegel. And when we do the history of philosophy, we endeavour to keep a philosophical point of view.

Now I don't want to give any idealized or glamorous image of the situation of philosophy teaching in France. Even though the idea may seem attractive, the reality is often quite dull. I remember reading the last interview given by Sartre, an interview in which he told his life-story as a high school student, and how boring and ridiculous his philosophy teacher was. I read that after my essay on women and philosophy was published, in which I had emphasized the fact that, in order to become a philosopher, you have to be cruelly disappointed by someone who should have been your mentor. Socrates and Descartes were the examples I gave, and when I read what Sartre had to say about his early years, I understood that he had been in the same situation, but I also realized that, in my article, in describing the positive role of disappointment, I had told my own life story as well.

RM: You mean you benefited from having a bad teacher?

ML: Before being taught philosophy at school, I had read various books: Pascal, Alain, Kant's ethical theory . . . enough in any case to think highly of philosophy. Then, for nine hours a week I had to attend the lessons of a narrow-minded, badly-read, sometimes comic old man. I did not like him, and he didn't like me either; I'm afraid I must have been a pain in the neck. But, looking back, I'm sort of glad I had such a poor teacher. Thanks to him I discovered the principle of equality; I mean this – in philosophy hierarchy doesn't matter, because no social hierarchy is relevant when rational debate takes place.

It doesn't matter that someone is the teacher and the other the beginner, for when the beginner is convinced that he or she is right, and the teacher wrong, then the beginner starts understanding what philosophy is, in other words beginning to grasp what it is to think by oneself, and how necessary it is to think by oneself. You may consider this to be a counsel of arrogance; it is rather a counsel of freedom and responsibility. I don't pretend I'm a self-taught person, however. The next year, working for the examination to enter the Ecole Normale Supérieure, I did have a good teacher, efficient, well-read and intelligent. But, fortunately, it was too late for me ever to become a disciple. Later, at the Sorbonne, I became a student of the moral philosopher Vladimir Jankélévitch, a remarkable and very kind professor, who did not want to have disciples, a man who was keen on students going their own way. In short, I have been lucky: I have had professors, books, but no mentor. Some authors have, of course, particularly influenced me, and among contemporary writers Foucault and Deleuze must be mentioned, I suppose, although I have never been a groupie of any of them.

RM: So you never had a mentor, or a *maître* as they say in French: it's an unusual thing not to have had a 'master' in France. What sort of figures did you identify with?

ML: I have friends with whom I talk. I always had – and this is central in my relationship to philosophy. I identify with my equals. As a child I had an absolute passion for Shakespeare, and I wanted to be a clown. I was more than fascinated, and I probably identified with those characters who were allowed to be impertinent to anyone; they were truth-telling, coarse-mannered, merry, melancholy, and profound – and also jokers. But the child found out pretty soon that life is not a play written by Shakespeare, no jobs for clowns are ever advertised by any royal court; and anyway, in Shakespeare, clowns are distinctively men. But when I discovered philosophy, it seemed to me so close indeed to the characters of Shakespeare that it could provide an approximate fulfilment of my initial wish. Jobs were available, and to women. It took me some years to understand that women were looked down upon in philosophy. To begin with, I was blind to that fact simply because the exclusion of women from philosophy was less blatant than in clownship.

By the way, another element delayed my realization of this: in the sixties, the final national examination, the *agrégation* I mentioned before, was not co-educational. Men and women didn't have to compete with each other: the State offered forty-five positions to women, and this gave a legitimacy to being a woman philosopher. The State was looking for forty-five women able to teach philosophy, and, as we all knew, they could be found easily enough. Each of us had to work hard to be among the forty-five because we knew that we had several hundred competitors capable of meeting the standards and demands. That kind of mutual regard and esteem made us partly blind to the fact that our male student companions thought women unfit for the remarkable subject that philosophy was.

You might think that I have forgotten the beginning of your question – what about my interest in the British philosophical tradition? Well, my field is British Renaissance philosophy and, as you said, it is not a very common field in France. But it is not so common in England either, I mean among philosophers. There are, of course, in Oxford, Cambridge or London, outstanding scholars who work on that period, but from the point of view of the history of ideas mainly, or literature. But my authors, Thomas More and Bacon, are completely neglected by philosophers. That's part of a wider problem in England, namely the lack of interest in the history of philosophy as such.

In France the same neglect may be seen as the result of something else: at the beginning of this century, various philosophical dogmas became established in the French academic world. The main one involved a simplistic worship of intellectualism, appraising the philosophical doctrines of the past according to the degree of value or hegemony they give to rationality. Because Kant intellectualizes more that Hume, Kant is thought to be a far greater philosopher than Hume. And, amusingly enough, a Kantian professor will look down upon his Humean colleague, but will in turn be looked down upon by any specialist of Hegel. Such an attitude leads of course to a definite contempt for the British Renaissance. So when I published a translation of Bacon's *New Atlantis*, with a commentary, no book by Bacon had been available in France for at least fifty years, except the *Essays*, which were read by specialists of English literature only.

May I describe myself as having a rather independent mind? Whether I have or not, my idea of rationality certainly does not involve the worship of any hegemony. British Renaissance philosophy was a fallow land to me, a field open to new exploration. And it was a fascinating time, I think, because philosophers were then freeing themselves from an age-long dominance of religion. Remember that, during the Middle Ages, the official doctrine had it that philosophy was but a humble servant to theology. A philosopher like Sir Thomas More, though a Christian, thought reason could have its own independent consistency, and its own field, namely politics and social organization. I consider it to be of interest to study such a form of rationality, which seeks its own independence without claiming superiority over all other forms of thought: according to these philosophers, the revealed truth of religion was still supposed to be higher. As I said before, we try to study philosophical systems of the past, keeping in mind present philosophical preoccupations. I'm trying to put forward some questions about the variety of forms of rationality – how different from each other those forms are – and a critical reading of British philosophers may be a good test. One runs the risk of being looked down on by everybody of course, but, since a woman is doomed to scant respect anyway, it does not matter. If you have nothing to lose, you can afford to be daring.

RM: A unifying theme of your work seems to me to be the *'imaginaire'*, the philosophical imagination. This is a difficult term to translate into English: it means both the capacity to imagine, but also the stock, or repository of images which colour philosophical discourse. And it's that side of it, I think, which has interested you particularly, that notion of the stock of images which are available in philosophy, or which perhaps even intrude in philosophy. Do you think that these images are an inevitable part of philosophy?

ML: I'm so glad you described the *imaginaire* as a unifying theme. Some people find it strange that I sometimes work on imaginary islands, utopias, or the idea of the island of reason, for example, and sometimes on the representation of women in philosophical texts. I can't see why they wonder, since it is one and the same approach in a sense. For what is called 'woman' or the 'feminine' in philosophical works is a fantasy, an imaginary being produced by the philosopher for certain purposes. Like all other images – like the image of the island, for instance. Let me take another example: Bacon says that there are three different kinds of intellectual attitudes, one being that of the ant, which gathers but does not work on what it gathers, the second being that of the spider, which builds up from its own substance, the third being that of the bee, which first gathers and then works it through. Now bees, ants and spiders function here as mere images, to lay out the difference between three kinds of intellectual attitudes, a difference which would not be easy to establish without the use of metaphors.

Bacon also says that nature is a woman, whom false knowledge deals with as if she were a prostitute, and whom true knowledge properly treats as its legitimate wife. A mere image this too, produced in order to emphasize a difference between two forms of knowledge, and assuming of course that the scientist is a male, and that to treat a woman properly is to father children through her. My work is about the stock of images you can find in philosophical works, whatever they refer to: insects, clocks, women, or islands. I try to show what part they play in the philosophical enterprise. But, obviously, when I work on the figure of 'woman', something more important is at stake than when I work on imaginary islands. First, because whatever a philosopher may write about islands, this will never do any harm to them, whereas what they say about women is generally an insult. As such, it has consequences. Secondly, because an average reader is prepared to acknowledge that what a philosopher writes about insects may not be a correct description of them, whereas anything and everything said about women is accepted without critical reflection. Recently I gave a paper on Bacon to an audience of people involved in the protection of the environment, and I mentioned the bees, ants, spiders, prostitutes and wives. A man in charge of our national parks protested during the discussion, along these lines: 'But ants are not like that at all, there are so many different species of ants. Some don't merely gather, but garden as well. Philosophers don't know what they are talking about . . .' But nobody stood up to say: 'But women are not like that at all. Some are neither prostitutes nor wives, and many wives are not decently treated.' I have come to the conclusion that insects are more protected against philosophical abuse than women.

You asked whether a stock of images, of pieces of pictorial writing, is an inevitable part of philosophy. I think so. First, because I have never come across a single philosophical system without images: even Kant, who is supposed to be an austere writer, has them. Secondly, I think that images play such an important part in a theory that no philosophical theory can do without them. In a sense they are the foundation of this or that system or way of reasoning; they organize the fundamental values of every system, they put forward, as it were, what is good and what is bad, and they express the differences the philosopher has to assume before getting started on his work. Nobody can object to the presence of myth and fantasy figures as such in philosophy. But I strongly object to the use of 'woman' as a construct of the imagination.

RM: I see that a recent article of yours discusses the idea of a dream of doctrine, a *somnium doctrinae*, in Kepler and Bacon. I recall a passage of Plato's *Theaetetus* where Socrates says he has had a dream: it always seemed strange that he should suddenly lapse from what seems to be ordinary philosophical argument into describing a dream he once had. It seems on the face of it irrelevant, an intrusion in the text. Philosophers aren't supposed to dream; they're supposed to come out with rational discourse. What do you think is behind this stratagem, if it is a stratagem?

ML: Any form of rational discourse proceeds from, or originates in, things which can't be sustained or produced through reason, things such as beliefs for example. In philosophy, these beliefs are set forth in the form of myths, or 'exempla', comparisons, images, or pictorial writing. But there is a contradiction here, since philosophy is also the assumption of a pure and total rationality: a philosophical discourse is supposed to appear as a self-grounded discourse [*auto-fondateur*]. This could be the origin of what you call a stratagem, namely the fact that no philosophical discourse can meet its own demands and standards. Day-dream and myth fill the gap, as it were, by providing the basic grammar of the system, by taking over from the conceptual work whenever there is a problem, and being sometimes ambiguous enough to support two opposite ideas at the same time.

Now, because philosophers are not supposed to be daydreaming when at work, excuses or pretexts had to be invented. The main one, I mean the one most commonly used by philosophers, is the claim of the educational technique. They say they use images to teach, because myths are easier to understand than concepts. It's as if images were translations of theories, theories translated for the ignorant, or for beginners, or for 'the mob'. This is what Bacon says about the Greek myths: the first philosophers, before Socrates, translated their theories into fables, because they were so new that it would have been impossible for people to understand them. Now, in the article you referred to . . .

RM: That's the one on the doctrinal dream.

ML: Yes indeed . . . I tried to show that Bacon is not talking about Greek myths at all, but about his own. The examples he gives can be seen as having a connection with Bacon's philosophy and the difficulties or impossibilities of this philosophy, mainly the problem of how nature is in contact with the divine.

However, excuses are necessary only when the author has to acknowledge that he uses a myth or talks about dreams. Which is seldom the case. We, the readers, have been educated not to pay any attention to the pieces of fantasy in philosophical texts, and such an education creates a kind of connivance or complicity with the classical authors. We read them as they ask to be read. Some years ago, when I started my work on islands, I described it to my friends, and asked them whether, if they came across an island, they would be so kind as to let me know. Then, for a conference on seventeenth-century philosophy, I took up the comparison you mentioned between Kepler and Bacon, and, I must admit, read Kepler for the first time. Now Kepler mentions Atlantis, Thule and Hesperides every now and then. A friend of mine is an expert on this scientist. 'Why didn't you tell me that Kepler is mad about islands?' I asked. 'I had never noticed', the expert answered.

In a sense we don't notice the images in a philosophical work, because we have been trained not to notice them, but also because images are quite invisible: they are often short, one sentence here, two lines there; they must look conventional or classical – and of course nobody will pay attention to a commonplace; and they are more or less consistent with standard ideology.

RM: Could you explain a little more this point about the hidden-ness of images, the idea that they appear standard, or normal?

ML: Well I'm trying to show that the philosophical *imaginaire* is specific: philosophy, as it were, has its own stock of day-dreams and myth. But on the other hand images must look as banal as possible, that is to say acceptable, that is to say invisible. They must look as consistent as possible with common ideology, though they are specific. Take sexism for instance: we do live in a sexist society, so, whenever a philosopher makes a sexist statement, the reader may take it as a matter-of-course remark. Now a closer look at any sexist fantasy – say in Sartre's *Being and Nothingness* – will show that it is not just standard sexism, but a special blend of sexism devised in order to sustain Sartre's system and hide its blunders. So you have to look at philosophical images in a dialectical way, since they are home-made, but seem imported.

It is not just by chance, perhaps, that a woman and a feminist undertook the critical analysis of what you call the stratagem. I could not read the remarks male philosophers make on women as an invisible matter-of-course. I always found them stupid and revolting, and far below the theoretical demands of philosophy. But none of the other images were invisible to me either, probably because a feminist is not prepared to take at face value any declaration of self-satisfaction, nor to understand anyone as he or she asks to be understood. Philosophers are supposed to come out with a totally rational discourse, and on this ground they claim a distinctive superi-ority over everything else; they claim philosophy is better than any other form of discourse, knowledge or creation. A feminist doesn't believe in such a thing, though she lives in a world where this attitude is common indeed. I'm not only referring to the fact that many men assume that they are, as such, superior to women; I'm also thinking of a feature of machismo, the fact that the macho man thinks he is superior to all men as well, and more 'male' than any other. As you may imagine, we are a bit sceptical about that kind of fantasy, and we are not keen on hierarchy anyway. Now philosophy tends only too often to be the machismo of the intellectual world, so let us show that it is not what it pretends to be, and has no claim to superiority over any other form of knowledge.

In order not to be misunderstood, let me add two things.

I said that such a thing as a 'total rationality' doesn't exist. Yet one can acknowledge that there are rational efforts in the work of philosophers, and valuable ones. And if the assumption of uttering a self-grounded discourse is seen to be a form of intellectual machismo, this need not imply that rationality itself is masculine. In fact, I doubt that we can really know what is 'masculine' and what is 'feminine' in the absolute sense. Of course we can identify certain attitudes and pretensions as phallocratic, certain yielding or submissive attitudes as linked to the oppression of women, and some critical points of view as a position that can be shared by feminists and men who know that it is a pointless fight, indeed, the fight about who is more male than one's neighbour.

RM: You identify two, or three, sets of attitudes there: firstly the phallocratic attitudes, and we know the kinds of images involved here – rationality, penetration, emotionlessness. Secondly, a set of deferring attitudes which, in sources hostile to women, is often linked to femininity: being submissive, accepting, being penetrated rather than penetrating, and so on. But you also identify a possible third type of approach.

ML: I suggested this threefold classification, instead of the age-old duality between the 'masculine' and the 'feminine', which seems to lead quite inevitably to the appalling mixture of images you just mentioned. Anyway, one should focus on social relationship, instead of differing natures; the duality of the masculine and the feminine should be replaced by this. And I must say I'm taken aback when I see contemporary philosophers use this simplistic set of categories, the masculine and the feminine. I thought that none of us believed any longer that such a thing as a 'substance' existed. Now when someone suggests that one thing is 'masculine' and another 'feminine', he is implying substantial qualities. I thought we had finished and done with any 'theory of the faculties': if someone says that reason is masculine, and intuition feminine, for instance, he's assuming that there are faculties, faculties so inimical to each other that they can't be part of the same subject. And when a male philosopher says of himself that he is partly 'feminine', in order to show that he is more complete than his colleagues, and so superior to them, what can this be? Alchemy? The idea that you can take the attribute of one substance to insert it into another substance . . . what philosophers say about the difference between male and female nowadays is archaic and unworthy of philosophy itself.

Now 'phallocratic' does not mean simply 'masculine' – it's masculinity in a situation of power. Submissiveness is not an equivalent of femininity, but the actual situation of women oppressed: so the third category, which I call critical feminism, would be the point of view of people fed up with oppressive relationships, namely feminists of course, but also men who don't want the traditional '*machiste*' role. If anything like a 'universal' is to be found, it can't be but in this third category – or rather, it will have to be created there.

SELECT BIBLIOGRAPHY

L'Imaginaire philosophique (Paris: Payot 1980); English translation: *The Philosophical Imaginary* (London: Athlone Press 1989).

Bacon: *La Nouvelle Atlantide*, followed by 'Voyage dans la pensée baroque' (with Margaret Llasera) (Paris: Payot 1983).

Shakespeare: Vénus et Adonis, followed by 'Genèse d'une catastrophe' (Paris: Alidades 1986).

L'Etude et le Rouet (des femmes, de la philosophie, etc. (Paris: Le Seuil 1989); English translation to be published by Basil Blackwell.

Articles

'Women and Philosophy', *Radical Philosophy* 17 (1977), 2–11.

'Irons-nous jouer dans l'île?', in *Ecrit pour Vladimir Jankélévitch* (Paris: Flammarion 1978).

'A woman divided', *Cornell Review* 2 (1978).

'De l'existentialisme au *Deuxième Sexe*', *Magazine Littéraire* 145 (1979), 49–51. Three English translations: Proceedings of the conference *The Second Sex Thirty Years Later* (New York University 1979); *I&C* 6 (1979), 47–57; *Feminist Studies* 6 (1980), 277–89.

'Utopias: scholarly', *Social Research* 49 (1982), 441–66, special issue '*Current French Philosophy*'.

'Quelle modernité philosophique?', *La Revue d'En Face* 12 (1982), 17–32.

'Bacon et les science humaines', *Le Magazine Littéraire* 200 (1983), 49–51.

'L'idée d'un "somnium doctrinae" chez Bacon et Kepler', *Revue des Sciences philosophiques et théologiques* 67 (1983), 553–63.

'Sartre ou l'unique sujet parlant', *Esprit* 5 (1984), 181–91.

'L'espérance dans la science', in *Bacon, science et méthode* (Paris: Vrin 1985).

'L'homme et la nature dans les jardins de la science', *Revue Internationale de Philosophie* 159 (1986), 359–77.

'Arts and women, of philosophy without borders', in *Contemporary French Philosophy* (Cambridge: Cambridge University Press 1987).

Jacques Derrida was born in Algeria in 1930. His early work, Plato's Pharmacy, *published in three sections in the journal* Tel Quel, *was to establish a style and a set of concerns. More orthodox philosophical papers, such as* Differance, *establish the intellectual grounds for the course which he now pursues. His links with French institutional life have been as innovative as his thought: he was a founder of the International College of Philosophy in Paris, and is presently attached to the Ecole des Hautes Etudes en Sciences Sociales, Boulevard Raspail, Paris. He is a critic of institutions, yet demands the standards and continuity which flow from them. Derrida looks towards German philosophy more than any other, and clues to his programme may be found in Heidegger, Hegel and Husserl. The major concern of his work is meaning and its relation to text: semiotics is particularly associated with his name, and this involves a theory of symbols, signs and meaning. His work has also been associated with the critique of the idea of the author.*

6

JACQUES DERRIDA

RM: You've been active in the Group for Research into the Teaching of Philosophy (GREPH). You know, I'm sure, that philosophy is not taught at all at the secondary level of education in Anglo-Saxon countries. I don't know whether it is because philosophy is considered dangerous, or destructive, or too difficult, but, whatever the case, philosophy is not part of the secondary school curriculum. And, with the assistance of this research group, you are proposing to extend, even in France, the teaching of philosophy, which is already quite widespread by the standards of other countries.

JD: Yes. The paradox here is that the Group was established in 1975 at a very specific point in the history of philosophical education in France. This said, in spite of the narrowness of this particular context, the aims of the Group are not restricted to France only. With regard to France, our concern in 1975 was to ensure that philosophical education in French high schools was safeguarded and protected, and also extended: France is one of the few countries to provide teaching in philosophy at high school level, but we wanted to see it taught *before* the final year. And we wanted to analyse the reasons behind the fact that for a very long time, in France and elsewhere, it was thought that philosophy could not be taught to students below the age of 16 or 17. And we wanted to analyse the presuppositions or prejudices, of a philosophical or socio-political nature, which lay behind this opposition to extending the teaching of philosophy to younger age-groups. These ideas are very old. Nevertheless the concerns of the Group were not limited to France itself. And the whole teaching of philosophy at university level, in the industrial world in general, was our concern. So the work of the Group was partly concerned with the French context and partly not. We did note that the activities of the Group were of great interest to philosophers from other countries: this was a pleasant surprise for us.

RM: I'm sure that would have been the case. Am I right in thinking that the teaching of philosophy at the secondary level in France is very much historical in orientation? You don't give a problem to the student to discuss as such, but you go at it through the study of the great philosophers and systems of thought.

JD: There is a debate over that very question within the French education system. Normally the programme for philosophy classes is couched in terms of general questions: action, thought, knowledge, ontology, ethics and so on; these issues are laid down. But it is true that many teachers insist on the need to study these issues on the basis of historic treatments: and I'm of that view myself. You can't settle these questions, in the absence of, not an historicist approach, but an historical approach, by taking into account the history of the problem, without allowing this process to become a doxography, a recital of opinions. The historical dimension is important. But there is a debate over this in the French teaching body.

RM: This way of doing philosophy on the basis of historical texts is perhaps characteristic of French philosophy in general . . .

JD: Of continental philosophy in general, I'd say rather. German philosophy, and Italian philosophy, are both more historicizing than Anglo-Saxon philosophy, I would imagine.

RM: I sometimes have the feeling that the great philosopher is the person who is incapable of being a good historian of philosophy, who crushes completely the philosophical sources which he reads. Would you agree with that?

JD: Not really. The great philosopher – this question of the great philosopher is also a difficult one, and in the GREPH we are in fact attempting to enquire into the means by which philosophers are legitimized as great philosophers. How does one become a minor philosopher, or how does a text become a major writing? Major texts have certain privileges, minor texts are dropped; these are issues which are very significant to us. In my view, what are called great philosophers are those who

94

have a very clear relationship to the history of philosophy, in some cases a relation of violence, since these are people who ill-treat the history of philosophy, so to speak. They use force to integrate the philosophers of the past into their own teleological schemas. Aristotle did this, Hegel did this, Kant also in a certain sense. So I think that 'great' philosophers are sensitive to historic treatments, not as classical historians of philosophy, respectful of what they read, but in a mode of thought which does violence, in the best sense of the word. Heidegger is historical in a sense, although this leads him to conclusions which are difficult for classical historians of philosophy to accept. So there is a problem there. But I wouldn't say that great philosophers are indifferent to the history of philosophy.

RM: Returning to the schools, and the fact that philosophy is not taught before the final year in France: what are held to be the explanations for this? Is it because philosophy is thought to be too hard for younger pupils, or too dangerous . . .?

JD: I think it *is* considered to be dangerous, though this may not be admitted. People do not say explicitly that philosophy is dangerous: they say that it is too difficult, that it is inaccessible to insufficiently trained minds, but in my view it *is* considered to be dangerous. Not just for political reasons, as has been said now and then, but one has the feeling that the nature of philosophical enquiry is 'transgressive', in relation to various norms and rules which are considered to be necessary for adolescents.

Looking at the question of level, since it is also said that philosophy is too difficult, and people like me and those in the GREPH think that philosophy should be taught earlier in the curriculum, it is true that teachers now are complaining, much more than previously, of the lack of training in language, logic and rhetoric of the pupils of today in comparison with earlier times. Philosophy teachers say that it is more difficult than it used to be because the pupils are coming to us with a lack of cultural training, weakness in the use of language, which makes the teaching of philosophy even more difficult than it once was. And I think that this is true to a certain extent, and that the same thing is true in other countries. The paradox is that we are asking that philosophy be taught earlier, whereas there are those who are asking that it be taught even later. At

17 or 18 they are not supposed to be sufficiently mature: their interest in philosophy, their use of the language, their logical ability, their rhetorical capacity are said to be inadequate.

RM: And on the ability of philosophy to corrupt people, am I right in thinking that French philosophy is associated in the public mind with anti-clericalism? It could therefore be thought dangerous.

JD: I don't think so. Probably some people see it that way, but I don't think that one can say that French philosophy in general is anti-clerical. Though it might be so to some people. They would say that philosophy is dealing with questions about God, ethics and politics in such a way as to disturb or pervert the established moral order, or even religion itself. I don't think this is true, but it is probable that this is the concern which is present.

RM: If we can move to your own thought: the idea of deconstruction, this is a term which is now much travelled, particularly in the United States, and which will no doubt travel further still. I would like to give you an example drawn from Plotinus for your response: Plotinus, the Neoplatonist, says, in order to explain his notion of abstraction and of aphairetic thought (according to which elements are removed from an idea to find its real kernel), that it is as if a sculptor before a block of marble begins to remove, through his art, bits of stone, piece by piece. In the end he finds the beauty of the form of the statue within the stone, by a process of removal. It's a type of negation, but one can scarcely call it negation: for him it's *aphairesis*, or abstraction . . .

JD: 'Subtraction' is also used.

RM: Yes. If I advocated this as a means of explaining the idea of deconstruction, would the analogy appear adequate to you?

JD: No. Though I am very interested in that, and in Plotinus, and I feel certain affinities between my own work and some Neoplatonic themes. One would have to be very careful about this however. Nevertheless the image you used, the image of abstraction or subtraction, which aims to restore an internal beauty or being which is hidden beneath appearances which must be removed, does not seem very close to what I am doing with deconstruction. First, deconstruction is not negative. It's not destructive, not having the purpose of dissolving, distracting or subtracting elements in order to reveal an internal essence. It asks questions about the essence, about the presence, indeed about this interior/exterior, phenomenon/ appearance schema, all these oppositions which are inherent in the image you used. The question is about this logic itself. On the word 'deconstruction', which in my mind was intended to translate a word such as *Abbau* in Heidegger – *Destruktion* in Heidegger is not a negative word either – it's a matter of gaining access to the mode in which a system or structure, or ensemble, is constructed or constituted, historically speaking. Not to destroy it, or demolish it, nor to purify it, but in order to accede to its possibilities and its meaning; to its construction and its history. And on this I don't think that the image as you presented it is at all analogous. This said, what there is in Plotinus of the movement beyond being, for example the *epekeina tes ousias* which gathers up in Plotinus a certain tradition of Platonic ideas, the issue of moving beyond being, is something which interests me greatly. I think that deconstruction is also a means of carrying out this going beyond being, beyond being as presence, at least. So this whole tradition of thought which goes from the expression *epekeina tes ousias*, beyond being, from Plato's *Republic* through Plotinus to a certain Heidegger, this whole tradition lies behind the notion of deconstruction though it is not absolutely coextensive with it.

RM: Plotinus also speaks about presence, the mode of being present, somewhat in Heidegger's manner; the word *paresti*, for example. The word dissemination: what's the force of this term as you use it?

JD: The intention of this term is to emphasize the force of multiplication and dispersion, or of differance, a force which doesn't allow itself to be gathered or totalized. It is not purely multiplicity, but in any case it's a differance which doesn't allow itself to be entirely brought together, totalized. And moreover it is a principle of multiplicity which is not merely polysemy: I distinguish in a number of places between polysemy and dissemination. Polysemy is a multiplicity of meaning, a kind of ambiguity, which nevertheless belongs to the field of sense, of meaning, of semantics, and which is determined within the horizon of a certain grouping, gathering together. Aristotle says that a certain degree of polysemy is acceptable, provided that it is possible to distinguish between different senses, and that the unity of meaning can be established. Dissemination is something which no longer belongs to the regime of meaning; it exceeds not only the multiplicity of meanings, but also meaning itself. I attempt to read the movement of this dissemination in the text, in writing; it can't be dominated by either the semantic or the thematic field.

RM: Dissemination means a kind of scattering . . .

JD: Which also bears a relationship to the generative, the seminal . . .

RM: Yes, the seminal, and the dis-seminal in dissemination? Dis?

JD: The differance in the seminal, not in the semantic . . .

RM: There's no essence in a text, which hides itself mysteriously? An essence to be found, as the ancient allegorists thought, perhaps?

JD: I wouldn't say that there's no essence, but the essence is not the last word of the text. There's always a surplus established, a dissemination, in relation to the hidden meaning or the essence of a text, reserved within a text.

RM: And what is the role of the author in relation to this polysemy?

JD: The author can't hope to constitute himself as author by *mastering* this polysemy. The term 'author' suggests someone who produces his text, who brings it together within themes, theses, senses. From the perspective of dissemination, I would not say that there are no authors, but whoever bears the name 'author', to whom the legitimate status of author is accorded, is someone who is himself determined by the text, and is situated in the text or by the text. He's not in the situation of the creator god *before* his text.

RM: If we can talk about differance now: as is well-known, you've suggested another term, that difference should be written with an 'a'; can you hear the difference as it's pronounced in French?

JD: No, it can be read but not heard.

RM: That's an interesting thing in itself. It's an active notion, *differance*, isn't it? The term labels a process which takes place: there's nothing passive about it. So there's a type of linkage which takes place.

JD: In the texts which deal with this, I do emphasize that differance is productive; but also that it's neither active nor passive. It is more of the order of what is called the middle, in Greek grammar, neither passive nor active. It deconstructs in fact all the philosophical opposites which are based on this polarization of active and passive. *Differance* is neither passive nor active.

RM: But doesn't the -ance ending in French bear an active sense, like *souffrance*, or suffering – the participial form made into a noun?

JD: *Souffrance* is not an act though: it's the middle way. It's a way of forming a noun on the basis of the present participle: *mouvance, souffrance*, these are neither activities nor passivities. This is why I have this form of the word; this grammatical form appeared to me more appropriate to suggest what I wanted to suggest with the term 'differance'.

RM: Since differance provides for a kind of re-attaching between things, in a way it could be said that differance no longer has any connection with difference with an 'e'. Here I'm thinking of the classic problem of the same and the different, from Plato's *Sophist* onwards: differance with an 'a' seems to take us in the direction of the same, in contrast with difference with an 'e'. The separateness of things seems somewhat mitigated.

JD: I think that you're right to say that differance, with an 'a', veers towards sameness. To take an example, the classical question of nature versus culture: saying that the relationship between the two is one of differance, with an 'a', means that culture is *only* nature differed (*différé*), with a delay, with this detour via a delay. This is what I call the economy: economy is in a way an idea based on sameness, the *oikos*, that which remains within the 'home' of the same. But I would stress another dimension of differance, which is, by contrast, that of absolute heterogeneity, and therefore of otherness, radical otherness. The term 'differance' can't be stabilized within a polarization of the same and the different. It's at one and the same time an idea rooted in sameness, and radical otherness, an otherness which is absolutely radical. So I'd say that differance can't be enclosed either within the same, or the idea of the radically other, about which nothing could be said. It's an enigmatic relation of the same to the other.

RM: For the English speaker there is some difficulty with the word *différer*: it is ambiguous, and perhaps it is one of those undecidable words. There is the differing aspect, to be different in the ordinary sense, but there is also the sense of *différé* as 'broadcast' . . .

JD: It's untranslatable: you have in English to 'defer', or 'delay', 'postpone'; but differing in the sense of being distinct is also part of it, and the two don't go together directly into English. And this highlights the indissociability of what is said, and the language: untranslatability. There is a difficulty in isolating the sense independently of the language.

RM: Yes, and the notion of time is important with this term, isn't it? It has the sense of putting something off, and so differance produces in the reader a degree of expectancy.

JD: Yes, but here again I'd prefer to remove differance, subtract it, from any structure of opposites. So the temporal aspect, which I have emphasized, is there, but the temporal can't be opposed to the spatial. I often talk about spacing, but this is not simply space as opposed to time, but a mode of producing space by temporalizing it (*en le temps-poralisant*). Temporization, to temporize, means waiting or expecting (*attendre*), postponing or delaying. Temporizing is spacing, a way of making an interval, and here again with the idea of differance the ideas of spacing and temporization are inextricably linked. So time is not given priority over space.

RM: This reminds me of the Thomist idea of relation, which is defined as a movement *towards*. *Ad*, towards, the preposition itself practically becomes the relation. Difference in the Thomist system is the condition for the relation: it provides the space for the relationship to take place.

Turning to the question of desire, what *is* the role of desire in your system of thought? I ask the question because your idea of differance is relational and it goes somewhat in the direction of sameness. And when one looks at the idea of desire in, say, Hegel, or in the Platonic tradition with the idea of *eros* in the *Symposium*, and in the Augustinian tradition above all – Augustine is a great desirer – there is often a link with the idea of lack, and here one thinks of Lacan as well: in your thinking about the matter there seems to be no suggestion of desire as the result of lack, or as lack in operation.

JD: Yes, that's true. What bothers me with the use of the word 'desire', and I have often tried to avoid it, is that where the word appears in writers such as Lacan, and well before him too, it tends to be defined as part of the structure of the subject: of the soul, the psychological or psychoanalytic subject as we have it in Freud or Lacan. My concern was to develop a differance whereby desire was not seen as a matter of consciousness. If there is desire, it is *because* there is differance. This psychologism, this anthropologism bothered me. I have nothing against it in itself, but it is the idea of differance which interests me, and it is neither psychological nor anthropological. It's not tied to consciousness nor the unconscious nor to the psyche . . .

RM: Is it phenomenological?

JD: No, not that either, and in fact I attempt to put deconstructing questions to Husserl's phenomenological method, based on the idea of differance. So the idea of differance is neither psychological, nor anthropological, nor phenomenological, nor ontological, in a certain sense. Further, in the way that desire is used, as you noted a moment ago, there is a link established between it and the idea of lack or negativity. Deconstruction is not tied to the idea of lack nor to that of negativity: it is not dialectical either. For this reason I have always been most cautious with the word 'desire', though of course I consider that everything has to be explained by desire; but you can't give an account of desire without basing it on differance. There would be no desire without the structure of differance.

RM: So differance is the more fundamental?

JD: Yes, but the word fundamental bothers me, for the same reasons.

RM: At times desire is presented as a kind of motor which explains everything, if there's a rupture between this and that, as in the myth of Aristophanes, something has to . . .

JD: But it is a motor which is situated within the psyche, or at any rate within the subject, the consciousness or the unconscious, and that appears to me to be not radical enough. An account of this desire has to be given.

RM: So the analysis of desire must go beyond the subject.

In your *Plato's Pharmacy* you show that Plato held the written word in contempt, if I have understood you correctly, and that he held in high regard the spoken word or thought. And you show that his contempt for writing is more or less constant in western thought, and you talk about the sense of scandal that Plato seemed to feel over the fact that the word should undergo an incarnation in writing. I found the language you used here of great interest: 'the disgraceful intrusion', the 'scandal' of this event as Plato sees it. Further, there is said to be a kind of father–son relationship between the thought word and the written word. Could you comment on your language at this point?

JD: I wouldn't say that Plato feels contempt for writing. He himself practised writing, and what he says about writing in the *Phaedrus* is not solely hostile: he fears a certain kind of writing, that which is irresponsible, removed from the responsibility of the person who speaks, that which is emancipated from the father of the text, and which cannot respond on its own behalf. It is the abandoned word, that of reminding, rather than remembering, in Plato's words. It is the written trace for which nobody can take responsibility, the orphan; but there is a writing in the soul which is closer to the word, and Plato has nothing against this. He is not hostile to this writing. This said, the trial to which writing is subjected in the *Phaedrus* is regularly reproduced in the history of western culture, which is after all a writing culture. And from this there springs a series of paradoxes which I attempt to study: for what is to be feared is a dead repetition, a repetition of the word cut off from its source, and the question is whether this separation is inevitably damaging, or whether it can be avoided. Is there something in the structure of the word itself, a writing, which can be gone through, repeated immediately, and which can have the status of writing even in the oral form? These are the paradoxes which I attempt to consider in *Plato's Pharmacy* and elsewhere. But in *Plato's Pharmacy* I don't simply try to establish an opposition between word and writing, by claiming that Plato is for the word, and against writing. There are more complex things at stake in the scene concerning writing.

RM: And the word *pharmakon* with its two possibilities: in a sense Aristotle's school was more favourable to writing and took the initiative towards the establishment of libraries. They helped constitute the library for the Ptolemies in Egypt. And so do you consider it a prejudice or a tendency of western thought which gives preference to . . . is it to the spoken word, the vocalized word, or rather to silent thought, to internal thinking which could be verbalized?

JD: It's more than a prejudice: a prejudice is something that can be corrected or criticized, whereas this is something rooted in the very structure of western thought, which is tied to a certain type of writing, phonetic writing, which represents the spoken word by inscribing phonemes, and which is therefore a kind of signifier of a signifier. In a non-phonetic kind of writing the situation is entirely different: in this case letters are supposed to represent phonemes which themselves represent thought. So writing is doubly served, doubly instrumentalized: hence its servile character, on this view, and the threat of evil and negativity which can seem to be inherent in writing. But of course moving to phonetic writing represented great progress in the history of signs and the economy of communication: the west has always been programmed by what was without doubt progress in this area. So it's more than a prejudice, and because of this paradox there have been many contradictions and negations in the way writing has been treated in the course of the history of philosophy. Leibniz, for example, put forward systems of thought which were distinct from writing and which did not involve the alphabet, which could, in an economical way, designate simple ideas, and so he proposed a universal system which was not tied to the word. But behind this lay a whole set of ideas about the single thought, the philosophy of the mark or sign, which, if we had more time at our disposal, could be shown to belong to the same tradition.

RM: And the image of father and son in Plato's *Phaedrus*, the word and the writing: this masculine imagery is interesting. Do you think there has been a kind of masculinism at work in the structure of philosophy itself? I'm not talking so much about the social role of women in philosophy, or the fact that they have been excluded, although that no doubt contributes . . .

JD: It's not unrelated: even without doing the sociology of the history of women in the west, I think that the fact that there have been few women philosophers cannot be formally dissociated from this phallocentrism which we touched on a moment ago, and I have attempted to show that logocentrism, or phonocentrism, which is proper to western metaphysics, is also a form of phallocentrism. That's why I created the term 'phallogocentrism', to refer to one single structure of thought which both gives priority to logos and the voice, the *phone*, and to the masculine position in philosophy. I think this can be demonstrated, though it would be difficult to do it improvising here and now, but I've tried to highlight a connection between the statement of masculinity, the placing of a man in a hierarchical position over woman, politically, sociologically, philosophically, and ontologically as well, the connection between that and logocentrism. I think it's the same experience, the same history.

RM: And the Stoics also talk about the spermatic logos, and when you know that at the same time the Greeks believed it was the sperm alone which created life, whereas the woman merely provided the matter or the place for the life to grow . . . this becomes an image of great importance.

JD: Absolutely: the idea of form in Aristotle, for example, is regularly linked with the male.

RM: What is logocentrism exactly?

JD: Logocentrism, to put it in summary form, is an attempt which can only ever fail, an attempt to trace the sense of being to the logos, to discourse or reason (*legein* is to collect or assemble in a discourse) and which considers writing or technique to be secondary to logos. The forms which this has taken in the west are of course influenced by Greek philosophy. There is always, of course, the European ethnocentrism to bear in mind: it's not exactly the same thing as phonocentrism, though the two are often linked. You can have phonocentrism without logocentrism: for example, in non-European cultures the sense of the authority of the voice can be found, a kind of hierarchy which places the voice above writing. This is a thing which can be found elsewhere than in Europe. European phonocentrism expresses itself in logocentrism, by subjecting everything to the authority of the logos or the word. It's not a matter of creating an opposition between graphocentrism and logocentrism, or of overturning the hierarchy, but of questioning the very idea of hierarchy, of that particular hierarchy.

RM: In your view everything that's written is a sign: the word graphism is used, to avoid I suppose the idea of the simple word, to say something broader than that. Is there a category of words which have no other reference, which are what they are, having only the one meaning?

JD: Univocal? Well of course the critique of logocentrism is also a critique of the sign: it provides a critique of the signifier/signified distinction which has established itself in the western tradition, in the writings of Saussure. I'm not talking about a critique of Saussure in general, but of a certain Saussurean approach to the concept of the sign, and the subjection of the signifier to the signified, which led me to suspect the structure itself of the concept of sign. There are two possible tacks in the deconstruction of this matter: the first consists in recalling certain necessary characteristics of the sign. There is no thought without signs; Saussure said something of this kind. But secondly one can recognize within the concept of sign the characteristic mark of logocentrism. So there's a critique of the idea of the sign. This is why I prefer to talk about 'mark' or 'trace' rather than 'sign': with the idea of trace, the distinction between signifier and signified is no longer at all possible, and the distinction of the authority of the word, the unity of the word, is called into question. So in reply to your last question, I would say that there is no word in natural language, which carries in itself, in its connotations at least, a zone of symbolism which is irreducible. No word is absolutely univocal, transparent, whether it's the transparent representation of a sense or a signified.

RM: So this plurivocity has to be accepted, or assumed in your view?

JD: Yes, though I don't know about the need to assume that this is a sort of ethical rule; whether you assume it or not, it's there. It's there, and even if you don't want to assume it, it dictates your discourse irrespective of your wishes.

RM: What is the ideal form of philosophical discourse? In the Anglo–American philosophical perspective the ideal is often seen – there is an ideal I think – as the development of a purely philosophical rational language, purged of contradictions, and above all of ambiguities – a computer language, if you like, an apodeictic language. What do think of this ideal?

JD: Oh, I think that in the best of circumstances it's only an ideal: in fact it's an ideal which is inaccessible, and I'm not sure that it's a good ideal for philosophy. You mentioned computer language, language which is absolutely decidable. I don't know whether thought is of that order: the type of thought in which decidability in the computer sense is dominant would still be thinking. Nevertheless there is a history of computers, of an increasing complexity in computer science: what can be said is that what's called thought is not reducible to computers as they are constructed at the moment. Computers are in the end relatively simple, despite their apparent intricacy, but I don't want to make this into an attack on calculation, on machines: that would be a little too obvious.

RM: What is the future of philosophy?

JD: I have no simple answer to that. I'm not among those who say that philosophy is finished. Even when I talk about the closure of logocentrism, and the closure of metaphysics, I make a distinction between closure and end: I think that the conclusion that philosophy has reached its conclusion, come to its term, is a very dangerous thing and a thing which I would resist. I think that philosophy has, *is*, the future, but for the moment it has to give its consideration to that which has enclosed it, a set of finite possibilities. What does this finitude consist of? What is this finite element in philosophy? We have the feeling that philosophical discourse is exhausted, that it can only reproduce itself in different forms, in different combinations. What does this closure consist of? This is an opportunity for thought; it's nothing like death, or the end, but an opportunity. And if this is called philosophy, then I think that philosophy not only has a future but that it *is* only if there is a future, if non-anticipatible events lie ahead. What interests me here is the event, and the event is such only insofar as it cannot be programmed and therefore anticipated. That's what provokes thought. And that's what provokes philosophy.

RM: And of course you don't think that philosophy is an élite activity, which should be locked up in institutions. But what is the role of philosophy in society?

JD: I think that often, as a matter of fact, philosophy *is* reserved for élites: in any case it is not sufficiently accessible, available to the general populace, open, so an effort must be made to shift it, to move it to certain institutions, to *certain* institutions. I don't think it should be thought that philosophy can be

106

done outside institutions, in the wild so to speak. We need philosophical institutions to guarantee the tradition, the transmitting of skills, to learn to read traditional writings which are not immediately accessible; so institutions are necessary. One can't think philosophically without institutions. This doesn't mean that every institution is good, and that we have to content ourselves with the institutions at hand. My own relationship with institutions is very complex, with the result that what I do can appear in some respects to be anti-institutional, but this is rather a matter of working against a certain state in which institutions find themselves.

RM: You're willing to recognize that institutions have made some contribution to the history of philosophy?

JD: Absolutely: they're indispensable. Philosophy *is* an institution in a certain sense.

RM: What are you working on at the present time?

JD: For the last two or three years my teaching has been on the question of nationality, and philosophical nationalism. I'm trying to examine the way in which philosophy has linked itself to national self-expression, from the political, institutional, and linguistic point of view. Otherwise, I'm working on the notion of *chora* in Plato, the idea of place, the site, and the way in which this passage of the *Timaeus* is resistant to Platonism, perhaps even to Plato himself. And I link this question of 'place' to that of the city and of the nation, which I mentioned a moment ago. Otherwise I'm keeping on with the reading of Heidegger, and I'd like to bring out a book on Heidegger, which will also be linked to these issues, to the reading of Plato via Heidegger, to the reading of the *chora* through Heidegger.

RM: Yes, there is a kind of *chora* in Heidegger too, isn't there?

JD: The last writings of Heidegger are in effect a topology of being, so there's a conception of place, not of place in being, but of the place of being. Moreover when he alludes to Plato's *chora*, that of the *Timaeus*, it seems to me that Heidegger is somewhat reductionist: I'm not very satisfied by his reading of the *Timaeus*, nor of the question of place, and that's the area I'm working in.

RM: There's a very strong idea of the *humus*, a kind of foundation, in Heidegger, although he doesn't always want to admit it: he wants to dispense with it in relation to his idea of truth, for example, to dispense with the idea of truth as a foundation of sorts. You've always got the impression that with Heidegger there is a kind of soil, or earth . . .

JD: Yes, there is the soil, and the earth element, but at the same time there's also the idea of *Abgrund*, abyss, the bottomless. I think that it is too limited to take Heidegger's philosophy as a philosophy of foundations. There's a questioning of the idea of foundation which is rendered possible by the experience of the abyss, *Abgrund* and *Ungrund*.

RM: And are you able, on the basis of Plato's *chora*, to make connections with this set of ideas – of nation, and race? Because in the *Timaeus chora*, or place, is presented in the context of physics, and cosmology and so on.

JD: Well *chora* can have the very concrete sense of the place of one's birth, one's native land, village . . .

RM: But in the *Timaeus* it's specifically . . .

JD: Yes, that's right. And so I relate that extraordinary scene in the *Timaeus* about this place which is not simply one place among others, the place in which the demiurge himself inscribes the copies of the paradigms, to the use of the word *chora* in other passages in Plato.

SELECT BIBLIOGRAPHY

Of Grammatology, trans. Gayatri Spivak (Baltimore: Johns Hopkins University Press 1977).

Writing and Difference, trans. Alan Bass (Chicago: University of Chicago Press 1978).

Dissemination, trans. Barbara Johnson (Chicago: University of Chicago Press 1983).

Margins of Philosophy, trans. Alan Bass (Chicago: University of Chicago Press 1983).

Positions, trans. Alan Bass (Chicago: University of Chicago Press 1981).

Spurs, trans. Barbara Harlow (Chicago: University of Chicago Press 1981).

The Ear of the Other (Nebraska: University of Nebraska Press 1988).

The Archeology of the Frivolous, trans. John P. Leavey (Nebraska: University of Nebraska Press 1987).

Speech and Phenomena, trans. David B. Allison (Evanston: Northwestern University Press 1973).

Glas, trans. John P. Leavey and Richard Rand (Nebraska: University of Nebraska Press 1986).

Signeponge – Signsponge, trans. Richard Rand (New York: Columbia University Press 1984).